Knit One, Felt Too

DISCOVER THE MAGIC OF KNITTED FELT WITH 25 EASY PATTERNS

Kathleen Taylor

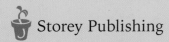
Storey Publishing

THIS BOOK IS FOR MY MOM, LONA PRATER,
WHO TAUGHT ME HOW TO KNIT, AND FOR MY GRANDDAUGHTERS,
ADDY JO AND SOPHIE, WHOM I HOPE TO TEACH.

The mission of Storey Publishing is to serve our customers by publishing practical information that encourages personal independence in harmony with the environment.

Edited by Gwen Steege and Margaret Radcliffe
Art direction by Cynthia McFarland
Cover and text design by Vertigo Design NYC
Cover and text photography by Ben Fink
Color consultant for knitted projects: Leslie Voiers
Illustrations on pages 7–157 by Elayne Sears and on pages 171–74 by Alison Kolesar
Text production by Jennifer Jepson Smith
Indexed by Susan Olason, Indexes & Knowledge Maps

Printed in Hong Kong by Elegance Printing
10 9 8 7 6 5 4 3 2

LIBRARY OF CONGRESS CATALOGING-IN-PUBLICATION DATA

Taylor, Kathleen, 1953–
       Knit one, felt too: Discover the magic of knitted felt with 25 easy patterns/by Kathleen Taylor.
              p. cm.
       ISBN 1-58017-497-3 (alk. paper)
1. Knitting-Patterns. 2. Felting. I. Title.
TT820.T36 2003
746.48'2043-dc21
2003050558

Contents

1

Honey, I Shrunk Your Sweater

I grew up in the Polyester Era, so I was middle-aged before I personally encountered the Shrunken Sweater Syndrome, though I knew a few unlucky souls who accidentally machine washed an expensive wool sweater with unfortunate results. I assumed that wool was delicate and that merely washing it made it shrink. But I've since learned that rather than the washing that causes the shrinkage, it's the combination of hot water, agitation, and detergent that causes the scales on the wool fibers to lift and adhere to each other. That adherence causes the fabric to contract, and that contraction causes the wool to shrink and become thick and fuzzy.

The Magic of Knitted Felt

Unplanned thick fuzziness can cause us to scream and tear our hair out, especially when we discover that a $400 cashmere sweater no longer fits anyone over the age of three. But once you've created that loose-knit, oversize object that you actually *intend* to shrink, you'll discover that you can use wool's natural shrinking ability to your advantage — and you'll become completely hooked on knitted felt. Taking control is not as difficult as you might think, as you'll soon find out when you knit your first project — and felt it, too. How you go about the felting process, the materials you use, and the length of time you agitate the wool all have a bearing on how the project shrinks.

Believe it or not, the floppy, oversized "bag" in progress on the left really will shrink down and shape up to look like the stylish hat on the right after being felted.

FIRST I DID IT THE HARD WAY

My very first knitted felt project was a wool roll-brim cap. Following the hints I found on the Internet, I used big needles to knit a hat that would fit a giant, and then dropped it into a sink full of hot, soapy water, and waited gleefully for it to turn into lovely, thick felt. I swished it around. I swooshed it around. I scrubbed and twisted and sloshed it until my hands turned to prunes. I worked on that hat until my wrists felt like they were going to fall off. As directed, I periodically plunged it into a bowl of icy water.

After forty-five minutes of intense labor, I had a really clean hat that hadn't shrunk at all.

I scrubbed some more.

I plunged some more.

I continued until I thought I was going to drop, and the silly hat still didn't felt.

THEN I DID IT THE EASY WAY

I asked around and was assured that if I continued scrubbing, the hat would eventually turn into felt. *Eventually* sounded like a very long time, so I threw it in the washing machine. I set the load for as small as the machine would allow. I set the water temperature to Hot Wash/Cold Rinse and added some detergent. I turned the machine on, and then I listened to some music while the washer did the work for me.

Of course, it didn't do the work all at once. After one complete washer cycle, I inspected the hat. Sure enough, it had shrunk some, but it was still way too big. So I washed it again.

After the second complete washer cycle, I checked again. The hat had shrunk even further, and it was starting to look more like fuzzy felt than soggy knitting. But it was still too big. So I washed it again.

Finally, after the third complete washer cycle, the hat was perfect! The formerly loose and floppy hat was now thick and fuzzy. The wool fibers expanded and wrapped around each other, locking together and creating a tight fabric through which no winter wind could blow. The colors had muted beautifully, and best of all, the hat fit perfectly.

It's all in the fibers: This drawing shows greatly enlarged wool scales prior to felting. During the washing process they will open, tangle, and close again.

. . .AND ONCE I EVEN TRIED IT THE SMELLY WAY!

Another term for knitted felt is *boiled wool.* So, in the spirit of another experiment, I tried boiling a hat on my stove. I used a big old canning pot that I'd found at a rummage sale. The heat and agitation of heavy boiling, alternated with plunges into a bowl of icy water, did the trick in about an hour.

It worked, but there were drawbacks. "What did you do," my husband asked, wrinkling his nose when he came home for lunch, "kill a sheep in here?"

There's no getting around the fact that wet wool smells like wet wool. And if you boil wool in your kitchen, your whole house is going to smell like . . . wet wool. Of course, if you felt the wool in your washing machine, you're going to get a little *eau de damp sheep* there, too, but it won't be as strong, or as pervasive, as when you simmer items on the stove. I happen to like the smell of wet wool, but I'm in the minority in my family.

In order to keep complaints to a minimum, it's best to do your felting in a room away from your family (mine never sets foot in the laundry room unless they're under duress). It's especially nice if you can have a door or some windows open during the process. Fresh air also helps to dry the wet felt. If you set your freshly felted things on a rack in the sun, they'll dry in no time.

You won't be able to tell, once the item is felted, whether you did the work by hand or with a machine, but your shoulders and arms will know the difference.

The Felting Process from Start to Finish

With experimentation, I found that items knitted with a particular type of yarn always took three complete washer cycles to felt. Further testing taught me that other yarn brands felted more quickly: Some needed just a few minutes of agitation, while others required one or two washer cycles. Each project, and each yarn, behaves differently during the felting process. One way to save water, time, and effort is to knit up several items and felt them together.

But whether shrinkage happens after five minutes of agitation, or three full cycles, felting knitted wool in the washer is absurdly easy. All you need is a washing machine set to wash in hot water, detergent, and a small mesh lingerie bag.

You'll find small, mesh lingerie bags in most grocery or hardware stores.

IT'S IN THE BAG

A mesh lingerie bag is an essential felting tool. No matter what yarn you use, knitted felt shrinks more in length than in width. However, wet wool is very heavy, and knitted items have a tendency to pull out of shape during agitation — sometimes with disastrous results. Large projects can, if unsupported, wrap around the agitator and stretch during the felting process.

One of my early failures was a knitting tote that ended up about a foot high and three feet wide, with felted handles that were fully twelve inches longer than they were when I started. I never felted another free-floating project. Placing the items to be felted in a lingerie bag helps to keep the tension on the wet yarn to a minimum, and allows for much less distortion during the felting process.

Knitted Felt in Seven Easy Steps

1. Toss the items (safely zipped in a mesh lingerie bag) into the washer.

2. Add enough laundry detergent or no-rinse wool soap for a small washload.

3. Set the cycle to the smallest size load and Hot Wash.

4. Close the lid and turn the machine on.

5. Check the felting process every few minutes, especially the first time you felt a new yarn. To check the progress, simply open the washer, stop the agitator, reach in (wearing rubber gloves if you want, since the water will be very hot), pull the lingerie bag from the soapy water, and look at the items. If they're as small as you want them to be, remove the bag from the washer. If the items are not fully felted, put them back in the water and set the machine to begin agitating again.

6. When the desired amount of felting has occurred, gently hand-rinse the items. To minimize the risk of further shrinkage, use rinse water that is no colder than the wash water.

7. Remove excess water by spinning the item briefly in the washer for no more than a minute or two, and/or rolling it in a bath towel.

Some yarns felt very quickly (one sample project for this book became almost too small within five minutes), while some yarns take several complete wash cycles. Experimentation and swatching will familiarize you with your yarn's propensity for shrinkage. It is especially important to swatch if you don't know the yarn's for shrinkage. See pages 12–15 for important information about how to swatch.

Animal fibers other than sheep's wool, such as mohair, llama, angora, and alpaca will also felt, so yarns spun from those fibers, or blends of those fibers with wool, are suitable candidates for felting. Several of the patterns in this book take advantage of the extreme fuzziness of felted mohair.

You may run across wool yarns that are specially treated to resist shrinkage and felting. Since knitted felt *needs* to shrink, do not use any wool yarn that is labeled "superwash" or "shrink-proof" for the projects. Yarns that are wool blended with acrylic may be shrink-resistant as well, although yarn with a small percentage of manmade fibers sometimes felt. In all cases, swatching is recommended.

Some pure white wool yarns resist shrinkage because the scales that cause felting were removed or damaged as the yarn was bleached. Off-white yarns seem to felt well, across the board, and not all white yarns resist felting, so swatching is essential before beginning a large project.

Front Loaders

Most yarns need at least one full cycle to felt, so you can felt in front-loading washers as long as you test a swatch first.

IS IT DONE YET?

Some people like their felt to retain some stitch definition, while others prefer fabric in which the stitches have shrunk enough to become invisible. If your goal is a completely soft and fuzzy surface, you can gently go over it with a pet brush after it dries thoroughly. This light brushing fluffs up the surface fibers and creates a well-finished, professional result.

Felt's percentage of shrinkage is not set in stone. Some wool yarns shrink more, and shrink faster, than others. As a general rule, knitted felt loses 15 to 20 percent in width, and 25 to 40 percent in height. *You* control the shrinkage: By halting the felt-

Shaping Up

Once you've felted your item, you'll need to shape it. If you want a hat to have a rounded crown, you may be able to simply smooth the wet hat into the proper shape and allow it to dry. Felted wool is a sturdy fabric, and it will hold its own shape fairly well without interior support. If you wish, place the hat over an up-turned bowl, canister, or any other item that is the proper size. If the mold you use for blocking isn't waterproof, cover it with plastic wrap before draping it with wet wool. Most small items will dry to a perfect shape if you smooth them out on a flat surface. For a really professional appearance, it's best to use pins to block and hold the felt in the desired shape. Don't be afraid to give your felt very firm tugs to get it into the shape you want it. You'll find it's quite tough and, while still wet, usually very malleable.

Practice patience, because it can take two days for a felted item to dry indoors. You can hurry the drying process along with a portable hair dryer. Clothes dryers are riskier: Felted items are likely to shrink further, and you can't control the item's shape if it's in a dryer.

If, when dry, your shaped and blocked item doesn't suit you, just wet it down and try again.

For best results, pin felted items to a sturdy blocking board until they are completely dry.

SOMETHING I LEARNED THE HARD WAY

Putting a pair of old jeans in the washer speeds the felting process because the extra bulk adds to the agitation. You may be able to eliminate a complete wash cycle, and thereby save wear and tear on the machine (not to mention water). However, be absolutely certain that the item you add to the mix does not shed lint, because said lint will automatically, and almost permanently, be integrated into the felt as it shrinks. Believe me: It takes hours to pick felted lint out. Ditto tissues inadvertently left in jeans pockets.

Do I Have Really Have to Swatch?

I know, I know. You've dutifully read each page so far, you have your yarn and your needles, and you've chosen a design. You want to knit! But there's one more thing you need to do before you can start: You have to knit a swatch. I completely understand your reluctance to bother. I'm a fly-by-the-seat-of-my pants sort of knitter myself. I prefer to figure out my gauge as I knit. But worse than taking the time to make swatches is wasting time and materials on projects that just don't work. And unlike other knitting projects, once the item is felted, you can't just pull out the yarn and start over. The fibers are irrevocably altered and completely locked together.

Loose Living

Remember that knitting destined for felting is loose and therefore somewhat hard to measure accurately (the measurements given in this book are approximate).

I confess that I learned the must-swatch lesson the hard way when I was designing the prototypes for this book. Some of the yarns I chose called to me so strongly that I threw caution to the wind and skipped the swatch altogether. But after several spectacular failures (a hat that should have fit a toddler but which felted too small for an infant, a Christmas stocking whose red body stained the white top, an expensive yarn that didn't felt at all, and a couple of other un-usables), I surrendered. I can't stress this rule enough: **Always** felt a test swatch of any new yarn before you begin a project.

WHY SWATCHES MATTER

A test swatch isn't necessarily an accurate indicator of how a larger piece knitted from exactly the same yarn will behave during felting. But a felted test swatch will tell you three very important things: (1) whether or not your yarn will felt, (2) how much it will felt, and (3) whether or not the colors are stable.

There are more subtle influences as well: If you give five knitters the same yarn and instructions, you'll still end up with five different-sized swatches. Each knitter works with a slightly different tension: My swatch knitted on size 10 needles could be the same size as your swatch knitted with size 11 needles. Different washing machines felt differently. Hard or soft water can affect the felting process. And even if everything else is uniform, different yarns, different colors of the same yarn, and even same-colored yarns from different dye lots, can felt differently. Personally, I think the surprises are what makes knitted felt such fun. To keep disasters to a minimum, however, it is essential that you knit a test swatch using each project's specified yarn, incorporating all of the colors and strands, before you begin a felting project.

Swatching Know-How

A swatch must be big enough to measure your knitting gauge, as well as the before-and-after size difference. Here's how to do it: Using the needle size and yarn specified in the pattern (or a substitute yarn of equal weight), cast on 20 stitches. Work 30 rows of stockinette stitch (knit 1 row, purl 1 row). Bind off.

If you are testing several colors for a single project, knit your swatch using bands of those colors, with a couple of rows of a neutral color as a spacer. If your pattern calls for doubling your yarn (either the same yarn or a worsted, for instance, worked along with a strand of mohair or blending filament), knit your swatch accordingly. If you have several yarns to test, you can felt all of the swatches in the same batch.

Flatten the knitted swatch on a hard surface (the edges of stockinette stitch will roll) and measure the number of stitches along a 2-inch (5cm) area in any row. Then measure the number of rows in a 2-inch (5cm) area. A needle gauge with an L-shaped opening cut into it makes measuring easier.

If your knitted gauge is *tighter* than the gauge listed in the pattern (in other words, you get more stitches per inch than the recommended gauge), re-knit your swatch using larger needles. If your knitted gauge is *looser* than the gauge listed in

Use a flat ruler to measure the number of stitches and rows in 2" (5cm).

the pattern (you get fewer stitches per inch than recommended), re-knit your swatch using smaller needles.

While matching the pattern gauge doesn't guarantee that your finished item will felt to the exact size listed, it has a much better chance of doing so if the gauges are the same. When the gauges match the pattern gauges, measure the width and length of the whole swatch and write those measurements down.

FELTING THE SWATCH

Although you don't have to weave in the tails on the swatches before felting, it's best to trim them, because tails have a tendency to felt to each other and create a real tangle (which will also be felted).

Place all of your swatches in a small mesh lingerie bag and wash according to the instructions on page 9. Check the felting progress frequently, because some wool yarns felt within five minutes. Be sure to check the felting of the first swatch made with an unfamiliar yarn at five-minute intervals, so that you can monitor the shrinkage accurately.

Don't be surprised if the samples don't shrink in one wash, or even after two washes. However, if you wash your swatches three or more times, and they show no shrinkage at all, you can be pretty certain that that yarn won't felt.

Record the type of yarn used, along with wash time and pre- and post-washing measurements.

WHAT A SWATCH WILL TELL YOU

Swatches will tell you whether your yarn is colorfast and actually shrinks at all, as well as how long it takes to felt it. Timing is especially important. Note any tendency to shrink very quickly, so that you can frequently monitor any felting you do with that particular yarn. With some yarns, fifteen minutes can be the difference between a hat that fits a teenager and one that fits a baby.

A swatch will also tell you how thick your knitted felt piece will be. Single-strand felted pieces are not as thick as double-stranded knitted felt. Certain items, such as tote bags and purses, may need that extra thickness for strength and stability. Some projects are double-stranded to compensate for the light weight of the original yarn. All swatches, whether worked with a single or a double strand of yarn, will shrink more in height than in width.

WHAT A SWATCH WON'T TELL YOU

A swatch won't necessarily tell you how a larger piece knitted from the same yarn will react to the felting process. Wet wool is heavy, and agitation can sometimes stretch the piece even as it shrinks (unfortunately, that's not a contradiction). Heavy, wide items, such as tote bags and purses, have a tendency to shrink much less in width than swatches knitted with the same yarn would indicate. The patterns in this book have been adjusted to take that propensity into consideration.

Long, narrow pieces may also stretch as they felt. If put into a washer unsupported, handles and drawstrings can end up longer than they were when you finished knitting them. Placing your knitted items in a mesh lingerie bag helps to alleviate these potential problems. The bag supports the wet wool as it's agitated, keeps items from getting wrapped around the agitator, and prevents the loss of small pieces.

Keep a Felting Journal

For each swatch, note yarn brand and name, color and dye lot, needle size, gauge, number of stitches and rows; pre- and post-felting measurements; and felting time.

What Do I Do with All These Swatches?

So, you've noted all the particulars of each felted swatch sample in your journal, and now you have umpteen fuzzy rectangles, in all sizes and colors collecting dust around your house. If you're like me, you hate the very notion of throwing away things you worked on, but there's no reason to throw these away. Felt is fabric, and any fabric can be cut and sewn. You can, with a little work and ingenuity, put these felted squares and rectangles to work in any number of projects. Before you begin, separate your swatches by thickness. Unless you want noticeable texture changes or thin pieces for appliqués, swatches of consistent thickness usually work best. Now, read on for some simple and practical ways to use your swatches.

MUG RUGS AND COASTERS: Select any swatch that is wide and long enough to fit under a cup or glass. Measure and trim the swatch so that it is square; brush the edges to disguise the trim. If you wish, work an embroidered or single crochet edging around the coaster in a contrasting color. Make the coaster waterproof by painting the underside with a non-skid plastic coating, such as Plasti-Dip. (See below left.)

HOLIDAY ORNAMENTS: Using a permanent marker, draw around any holiday cookie cutter that will fit on the swatch. Cut just inside the drawn line. You may work a contrasting-color edging around the outside of the ornament in embroidery or single crochet. To make a hanger, thread a length of pretty ribbon or cord in a large-eyed needle and sew through the center top of the ornament. (See below middle.)

SACHET PILLOWS: Place two matching or complementary colored felted pieces together, wrong sides facing. Using matching thread, machine- or hand sew the pieces together about ¼" (.6cm) from the edges, leaving a small opening. Stuff it with sweet-scented potpourri and a bit of polyester fiberfill; sew the opening closed. Our example is decorated with a small felt ball. (See below right; for felt ball instructions, see page 157.)

This coaster set tested alternating rows of worsted and a novelty yarn/worsted mix.

Christmas "cookie" trees are decorated with brightly colored perle cotton French knots.

Dried lavender, rosemary, and crushed rose petals are good choices for sachets.

Keep your cell phone safe at hand in a soft felt case with a fast-release clip for belt or purse.

For a touch of glamor, use felted luxury yarn for an eyeglass case suitable for evening wear.

This bold retro patchwork design is large and sturdy enough to use as a floor pillow.

CELL PHONE CASE: Place two swatches together, wrong sides facing. Our example is about 4½" x 6½ " (11.5 x 16.5cm), with the top layer about ¼" (.6cm) smaller than the bottom layer. Using matching thread, hand or machine stitch along one short and both long sides. Attach a purchased quick-release fastener to one corner. (See above left.)

EYEGLASS CASE: Fold a 7½" x 5½" (19 x 14cm) felted swatch so that the short edges come together at the middle (this seam will be at the center back). Whip-stitch the center back seam and the bottom seam. Attach a purchased chain or bead necklace at the upper corners, so that you can wear it around your neck. (See above middle.)

PATCHWORK PILLOWS: Lay an assortment of swatches on a piece of fabric cut to the size of your pillow form. If necessary, trim the outer edges of the swatches so that they fit neatly together and the outside edges are even. Pin, then baste the swatches in place. Machine zigzag along the edges of each swatch.

Lay the finished pillow top on backing fabric, right sides together. Cut backing to match pillow top. Pin pillow top to backing, and hand or machine stitch around three sides, using a ½" (1.25cm) seam allowance. Trim excess fabric from seams and corners. Turn right-side out. Slip a ready-made pillow form or polyester fill into the opening. Turn raw edges in; whipstitch opening closed. (See page 17 right.) You can make patchwork placemats using the same technique. Embroider or single crochet an edging around the mats. Make mats about 12" (31cm) by 16" (41cm).

QUILT SQUARES: Cut pieces of any small patchwork quilt pattern out of felted swatch fabric. Trim off the recommended seam allowances and fit pieces together on a flat surface. Whipstitch pieces together. Flip the square over, and whipstitch again for reinforcement. Use the finished quilt squares as pillow tops or a shopping bag, or assemble enough squares to make a small felted throw.

EMBELLISHMENTS: Any felted item, such as a pillow top, hat, slippers, bag, or mittens, may be embellished with felt appliqué, either before or after felting. (For instance, see the Wine Sack on page 143.) Use a cookie cutter, or trace or create your own pattern to cut shapes from felted swatches. Before attaching the appliqué, you may want to embroider or crochet around the outside edges with a contrasting color thread or yarn or liven it up with beads, ribbon, buttons, embroidery, or needle felting. Sew appliqués in place with matching or contrasting thread or yarn, as you prefer.

The Portable Craft

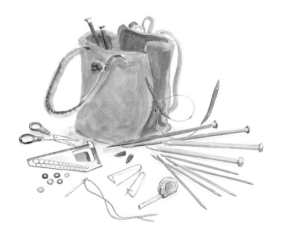

When you're knitting, you can carry everything you'll need to keep you occupied in a regular handbag, or treat yourself and make a roomy felted bag. The Lunch Bag Carryall (page 33) would serve the purpose well. In addition to your knitting needles and yarn, you'll also want a ruler, a pair of scissors, a yarn needle (which is blunt tipped and has a large eye), stitch markers big enough for large needles, and a medium-sized stitch holder (similar to a large safety pin, used for setting live stiches aside for future use). You might also find a stitch and needle gauge handy.

THE NEEDLES YOU NEED

There are only a few knitting needles sizes called for in this book, and all of them are large. You will probably want to have straight, double point, and circular needles, since some of the patterns require more than one style. Most of the patterns call for 10" (25cm) straight needles; you may sometimes need 14" (35cm) needles. Double point needles come in short and long for most of the necessary sizes. A 16" or 18" (40 or 45cm) long circular needle works well for these projects.

Most of the patterns in this book using worsted weight, single-strand yarn call for US size 11 (8mm) or US size 13 (9mm) needles. Most patterns here that use bulky weight, single-strand yarn call for US size 15 (10mm) needles.

THE SCOOP ON KNITTING TERMS AND TECHNIQUES

The knitting called for in this book is extremely basic. Beginning knitters should have no problem with most of these patterns, and experienced knitters will find all of the projects to be quite easy. Many of the little details that matter in regular knitting, such as different cast-ons or bind-offs, or the slant of an increase or a decrease, usually disappear completely when the item felts. Use whatever cast-on you like. Ditto with bind-offs, increases, or decreases. If you need help with basic stitch definitions or techniques, refer to pages 171–174 for guidance.

It's Okay to Substitute—Usually

Many of the patterns in this book call for specific brands and colors of yarn. You may substitute different brands of the same weight yarn, so long as you remember to test swatch everything. You may also use any yarn colors you please, including those you have dyed yourself. Please bear in mind the caution about some pure-white yarns not felting well, and choose off-white or cream color yarns for dyeing. Experiment with patterns and colors, and have fun!

From Sow's Ear to Silk Purse: Troubleshooting

No matter how much experience you have as a knitter, felter, or designer, you're going to experience an occasional failure. I had been knitting and felting hats, slippers, and purses for a couple of years before I wrote this book. One of my first book projects was a large knitting tote. Having felted smaller items with that particular yarn many times, I confidently worked out the pattern based on the purses I had knitted and felted previously. I then spent two weeks knitting a gargantuan bag. When I took the bag out of the washer, I was horrified to discover that it had lost almost nothing in width, but had shrunk down to not quite a foot tall. As a tote bag, it was useless. I said many bad words, chalked the disaster up to experience, but couldn't quite bring myself to throw the bag away. The bag may have been unusable as a tote, but it had more than enough fabric to cut and sew four matching pillow tops, with plenty of scraps left over to make matching coasters!

Small Is Beautiful

If all else fails, give a too-small item to a smaller person or cut it up and use the pieces to make one of the swatch projects on pages 16–18.

IT'S TOO SMALL

Okay, you made your swatch, you followed the directions, you checked the felting process carefully, but the finished item still turned out to be too small. Don't throw it away. First, see if you can stretch it out to a usable size. (See Too Much of a Good Shrink on facing page). If too-tight Fair Isle strands on the back are the culprit, try clipping each float and stretching the item again. (Because it's felted, the knitting will not unravel.)

IT'S TOO LONG

If a felted bag, purse, or hat is too long, evenly trim the excess. The edge won't ravel, so you don't need to hem it, but you may wish to give it a blanket-stitch edging with contrasting yarn. If purse handles are too long, trim the excess, then re-attach them and sew decorative buttons on the overlap. If the foot of a slipper is too long, trim excess, sew toe closed, and brush the seam to hide it.

Try washing too-big items again. I have not done any scientific research on the subject, but early on in my felting experiments I ran some of my less-successful pieces through many wash cycles in the machine, just to see how small they would actually get. Eventually, all of the pieces reached a point where they stopped shrinking. This makes sense when you remember that felt is nothing more than permanently matted fibers — they can only compress so far without the help of special machinery. I also learned that there was no set number of felting cycles to reach that point. Some yarns reached maximum shrinkage in four cycles, others took eight. If your item is still too big after three or four wash cycles, try a couple more. Another felting might just do the trick.

If the opening of a purse or pair of slippers is baggy even after additional felting, try running a line of gathering stitches around the edge, using unfelted yarn, thread, or narrow elastic. Another option is to knit and felt an I-cord for a drawstring, and then cut evenly spaced eyelets around the edge of the opening. An

Too Much of a Good Shrink

Remember that felting knitted wool (or *fulling,* as it is also known) is an art, not a science, and variation is not unusual.

If a felted hat, slipper, or pillow is smaller than expected, you can often stretch it. Wool felt is an amazingly strong fabric and nearly impossible to tear. You won't be able to make the item as big as it was originally, but you should be able to increase its size by 10 to 15 percent.

First, wet it thoroughly. A felted item freshly removed from the washer is wet enough, but if it has already dried, soak it in warm water for at least a half hour. Squeeze out the excess moisture, and then get a good grip on each side and pull with all your might. By judicious stretching, it's possible to make the hand of a mitten wider without pulling the cuff out of shape. It's easy to make the foot of a slipper longer without enlarging the opening. It's simple to make a floppy hat brim lie flat without distorting the crown. If possible, try the wet item on before you set it aside to dry, so that you can stretch it some more if necessary. When it reaches the desired size, smooth it into shape and allow it to air dry.

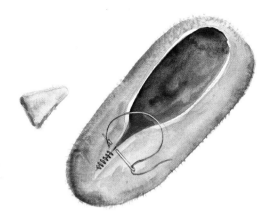

advantage of felted knitting is that you can trim it or even make holes in it without fear of tearing or raveling. The new eyelets will appear to have been knitted in.

If the opening is too big to gather, you can cut the felt, remove the excess fabric, and whipstitch (do not overlap) the opening closed with sewing thread. After the seam is sewn, use a hairbrush or pet comb to raise the nap of the felt to make the seam nearly invisible.

You can also fold a pleat in a too-big opening. Tack the pleat down and sew a decorative button on it. Tell everyone that you did it that way on purpose.

To make a slipper opening smaller, cut a pie-shaped piece from the edge, then whip-stitch cut edges together with matching thread, and brush to disguise seam.

IT'S CROOKED

Even properly supported items can become distorted during felting, but you can generally fix the problem. Stretch the wet item until you get all the edges, seams, color blocks, and stripes straight and square. Pin the item to a board and leave it until it has completely air dried.

If the outside edges of a pot holder or pillow top are uneven and stretching doesn't even things out, use a ruler to mark straight edges and square corners, and trim the excess. If a purse flap hangs oddly, stretch it while it's still wet. You may also be able to steam press the damp area into shape. If nothing else works, cut the flap off the purse, trim it evenly, and sew it back in place with sewing thread. Brush the seam to cover it up.

THE COLORS BLED

If you test yarn combinations in your swatches (see page 13), you shouldn't have to deal with surprises of this nature. But if it does happen, you may be able to use Rit Color Remover to take the excess color out. A quick dip in the solution (mixed according to the manufacturer's directions) is sometimes enough to remove excess dye from areas where it isn't wanted. A quick dip in Rit Color Remover will also fade some of the original colors, however, so you'll have to decide if that's a fair tradeoff for removing the discoloration.

The process of felting wool could reasonably be called Yarn Abuse. Repeated washing in hot water, coupled with vigorous agitation can cause even the most hardy dyes to wilt a little. If you felted a swatch of your intended colors, you should have a notion of how the yarn will behave under pressure. But if you're surprised (and disappointed) by the look of your finished piece, you can overdye it.

Follow instructions on the package of dye carefully. Be sure to stir the item frequently to help ensure even color absorption.

You can also try hand-painting your finished piece in order to add dye to specific areas. I must warn you, however, that you're liable to end up with colors bleeding into places where you don't want it. Practice hand-painting on a felted swatch before you tackle a big project.

To Dye For

If colors bleed, you can overdye the piece to blend the colors, creating a subtle, attractive variation in the overall design. Remove buttons before dyeing.

THE COLOR IS UGLY

It looked so pretty in the skein. And even the swatch looked fine. But the finished item is just too icky to live with. You can overdye the entire piece as it is, taking the original color into consideration when choosing dyes. Or you can remove as much color as possible with Rit Color Remover and then re-dye it.

The Care and Feeding of Felt

Felted wool items may be dry cleaned, especially if they have large stains. For everyday dirt, however, you can wash wool felt at home. Washing methods are similar to those you follow for all of your delicate hand-washables.

Although felt is created by heavy agitation in hot water, your finished, felted items should be washed gently and air dried. Use a mild detergent, or you may want to look for one of the new wool detergents, such as Wool Mix, which is

Away with Pills

If wear and washing have raised
pills on the surface of the felted
fabric, trim them off after the
item is fully dry.

available in lavender and eucalyptus scents. These detergents do not require rinsing and also work very well for the felting process itself.

Run a sinkful of warm water. Add a squirt or so of detergent and swirl the water a couple of times. Lower the item into the soapy water and let it soak for an hour or two. Every once in awhile, jostle the item a little bit to make sure that it's entirely under water. Very gently scrub any stained or especially dirty areas.

It's important not to stretch the felt, so leave the item in the sink while you drain the water. Press down with your hands to remove as much excess water as possible, then remove the item from the sink.

Run another sinkful of warm water. Lower the item into the water and gently swish it once or twice. Allow it to sit in the rinse water for 10–15 minutes. Drain the water, again leaving the item in the sink and pressing excess moisture out. Repeat this process until no soap bubbles appear when you lower the item in fresh water.

When the item is fully rinsed, you may wish to spin it in the washer (making sure that your washer does not spray cold water during the spin cycle). Be aware that some heavy felted items can become permanently creased in the spin cycle, so spin it for only a minute or two, or avoid this risky procedure. A safer method is to fold a bath towel or two around the item and press to blot out as much water as possible. Use more dry towels, as needed. Shape and block the damp item as you did when it was freshly felted, then allow it to air dry.

If gentle hand scrubbing does not remove stains, you may use any stain remover that is specifically rated for wool fabric. Follow the manufacturer's instructions for use.

PROLONGING THE LIFE OF YOUR FELTED ITEMS

Knitted felt is an exceptionally sturdy fabric, but like other knits, even felted items may stretch or show other signs of wear eventually. The secret to better wearing and looking knits is to add stabilizing features. Here are some tricks that will help keep your creations in service for a longer period of time.

STRETCHY SLIPPER OR PURSE OPENINGS. If openings stretch with use, stabilize them by sewing a band of bias tape to the inside of the upper edge.

WORN-OUT SLIPPER BOTTOMS. Slippers will wear much longer and better — and be safer — if the soles are covered with non-skid fabric. Outline the sole of your slipper, then use the pattern to cut the non-skid fabric slightly smaller than the outline. Whipstitch the non-slip sole in place or use double-sided fusible interfacing to attach it.

STRETCHY HANDLES. To strengthen knitted handles other than I-cords, sew grosgrain ribbon to the wrong side. If I-cords stretch with use, cut the excess off, and if necessary, sew the cord back onto the bag. Or see the technique used for the handles on the Lunch Bag Carryall on page 37.

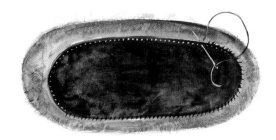

Make a pattern by tracing the sole of your slipper, then cut a matching piece from non-slip fabric about ¼" (.6cm) smaller all around. Whipstitch in place.

Look for the Silver Lining

HERE'S THE WAY TO MAKE A SIMPLE PURSE LINING:

1. Lay the purse on top of two layers of any lightweight fabric (with the fabric right sides together). Trace 1" (2.5cm) away from the outside edge of the felted item.

2. Cut the lining out on the traced line, and sew it together around the side and bottom edges, using a ¼" (.6cm) seam allowance.

3. Trim the corners and clip the curves, but do not turn the lining right side out.

4. Slip the lining into the felted item. Turn the upper raw edge under ¼" (.6cm), and slipstitch the lining into place. The lining will seem to be a little baggy, which allows for any stretching in the felt. You may want to tack the lining to the item at the lower edges.

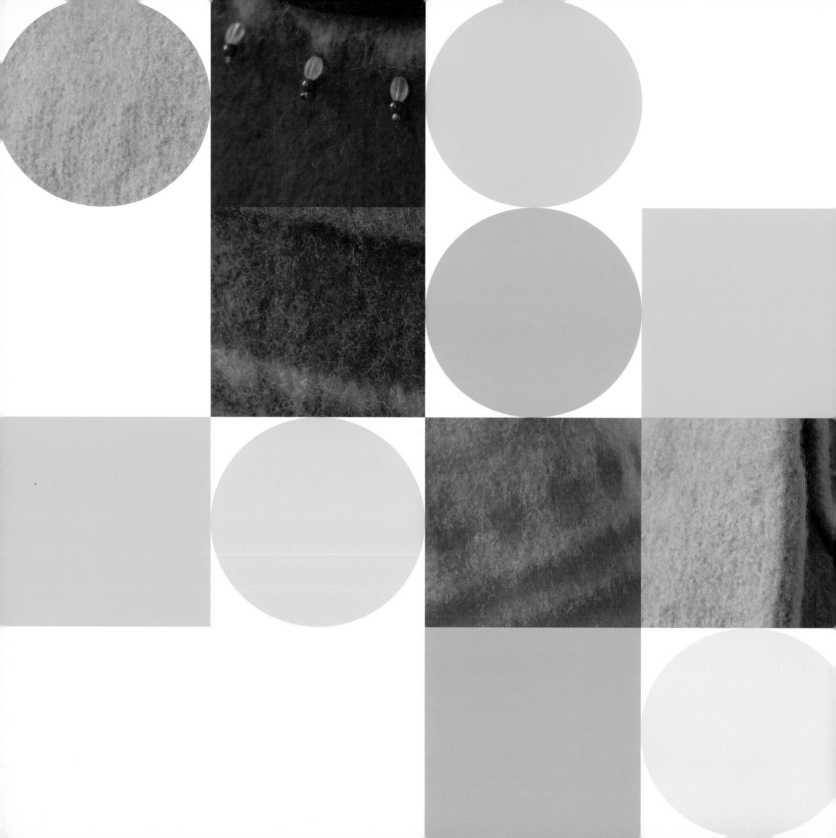

2 It's All in the Bag

An Evening Bag with Glitz

With all of the fascinating novelty yarns now available, your options are wide open when it comes to designing and knitting fun evening bags. This black bag gets its sparkle from a strand of metallic blending filament that is knitted along with the wool. Purchased beaded fringe stitched just below the eyelets gives the final touch.

YARNS

mc Brown Sheep Lamb's Pride, 85% wool/15% mohair, worsted weight, 190 yd (171m)/3.5 oz (100g) skeins
190 yds (171m) Deep Charcoal

cc Kreinik Metallic Blending Filament, polyester metallic thread with supporting core, 111 yd (100m) reels
2 reels Confetti Blue

NEEDLES

ONE SET US #11 (8mm) double point needles, *or size you need to obtain gauge*

GAUGE, BEFORE FELTING
7 stitches = 2" (5cm), 8 rows = 2" (5cm) in stockinette stitch

NUMBER OF WASH CYCLES TO ACHIEVE SAMPLE SIZE
One

OTHER SUPPLIES

Yarn needle, 1 package (36"/90cm) beaded fringe, 5½" (14cm) cardboard circle, matching sewing thread and needle

ABBREVIATIONS

cc contrast color
mc main color

APPROXIMATE MEASUREMENTS

Before felting

9" (23cm) wide, 9" (23cm) tall

After felting

9½" (24cm) wide, 7½" (19cm) tall

KNITTING THE I-CORD SHOULDER STRAP

SET UP	Using mc and cc held together, cast on 3 stitches.
	Following the instructions on page 171, knit a 48" (120cm) I-cord.
LAST ROW	Bring yarn around back of work, and knit 3 together.
	Cut the yarn, leaving a 10" (25cm) tail. Thread tail through a yarn needle, draw yarn through remaining stitch and fasten off. Weave end back up through center of I-cord. Repeat with tail at the other end.

KNITTING FROM THE TOP OF THE BAG

SET UP	Holding one strand of mc and one strand of cc, cast on 60 stitches. Divide stitches evenly among three double point needles. Join, being careful not to twist the stitches. (For information about knitting in the round, see page 173.) Continue to hold mc and cc together throughout.
ROUNDS 1–5	Knit to end of each round.
ROUND 6 (EYELET ROUND)	*Knit 4, knit 2 together, yarn over; repeat from * to end of round.
ROUND 7	Knit to end of round, knitting the yarn-overs from the previous round as normal stitches. *You still have* 60 stitches.
NEXT ROUNDS	Knit to the end of each round until the piece measures 9" (23cm).

DECREASING FOR THE BASE

ROUND 1	*Knit 4, knit 2 together; repeat from * to end of round. *You now have* 50 stitches.
ROUND 2	Knit to end of round.
ROUND 3	*Knit 3, knit 2 together; repeat from * to end of round. *You now have* 40 stitches.
ROUND 4	Knit to end of round.

ROUND 5	*Knit 2, knit 2 together; repeat from * to end of round. *You now have* 30 stitches.
ROUND 6	Knit to end of round.
ROUND 7	*Knit 1, knit 2 together; repeat from * to end of round. *You now have* 20 stitches.
ROUND 8	Knit to end of round.
ROUND 9	*Knit 2 together; repeat from * to end of round. *You now have* 10 stitches.

Cut mc and cc, leaving 10" (25cm) tails. Thread tails in a yarn needle and draw yarns through the remaining stitches. Fasten off. Weave in all loose ends on inside of work.

FINISHING THE BAG

Following the instructions on page 9, felt both bag and drawstring at the same time.

Set the bag flat on its bottom, smoothing it so its base is a circle roughly 5½" (14cm) in diameter. Smooth sides straight up and allow bag to dry thoroughly. When sides are dry, turn purse over to allow bottom to dry. Smooth I-cord evenly, stretching it to the desired length, and allow it to dry.

Place cardboard circle in bottom of purse to help it hold its shape. Trim the circle, if necessary.

Fold the tape that holds the beaded fringe in half lengthwise, and pin it just beneath the eyelets. With sewing needle and thread, use tiny back-stitches to sew the fringe in place.

Thread the I-cord through the eyelet holes. Tie the I-cord ends together at center front of bag. Tighten drawstring.

Lunch Bag Carryall

Inspired by a classic lunch bag, this sturdy carryall is big enough and sturdy enough for everything from knitting to lunches to yoga gear — or just use it as a generous-sized purse.

YARN

mc   Brown Sheep Lamb's Pride, 85% wool/15% mohair, bulky weight, 125 yd (114m)/4 oz (113g) skeins

350 yds (315m) Limeade (M120)

cc   Brown Sheep Lamb's Pride, 85% wool/15% mohair, worsted weight, 190 yd (173m)/4 oz (113g) skeins

cc A

60 yds (54m)   Limeade (M120)

cc B

15 yds (14m)   Lotus Pink (M105)

NEEDLES

ONE US #15 (10mm) circular needle, 16-18" (40-45cm) long, *or size you need to obtain gauge*

ONE PAIR US #11 (8mm) straight needles

ONE SET US #11 (8mm) double point needles

GAUGE

5½ stitches = 2" (5cm), 7 rows = 2" (5cm) in stockinette stitch with bulky weight yarn on larger needles

NUMBER OF WASH CYCLES TO ACHIEVE SAMPLE SIZE

Two

OTHER SUPPLIES

Yarn needle; 4 stitch markers; 8 yds (7.5m) waste yarn in contrasting color (preferably a cotton yarn); 5 yds (4.5m) 100% rayon, woven edge, washable seam binding, 9/16" (1.5cm) wide in a matching color; matching sewing thread and needle

ABBREVIATIONS

cc   contrast color

mc   main color

APPROXIMATE MEASUREMENTS

Before Felting

10½" (27cm) wide from corner to corner at base, 22" (56cm) high from base

After Felting

8¼" (21cm) wide from corner to corner at base, 12" (31cm) high from base

KNITTING THE BAG BOTTOM

NOTE	You will work in stockinette stitch (knit 1 row, purl 1 row) on a circular needle to create the flat bag bottom, turning after each row.
SET UP	Using mc and larger circular needle, cast on 26 stitches.
ROW 1	Knit to end of row. Turn.
ROW 2	Purl to end of row. Turn.
NEXT ROWS	Repeat Rows 1 and 2 until the piece measures 10" (25cm) from the cast-on edge. End at the completion of a knit row.

KNITTING THE BAG

NOTE	The bag is knit in the round. In this section you will pick up stitches along both sides and the cast-on edge of the flat piece just knitted. The pick-up is done with the wrong side facing so that a purl ridge appears on the right side of the fabric. This ridge will help you square up the base when you shape the bag after felting.
SET UP	With wrong side of work facing you, knit the 26 stitches. Place a stitch marker on the needle.
	Pick up and knit 20 stitches along one side of the bag bottom. Place a stitch marker on the needle.
	Pick up and knit 26 stitches along the cast-on edge. Take care to pick up the outside loop of the cast-on stitches, so that a single ridge of stitches shows on the right side of the bag. Place a stitch marker.
	Pick up and knit 20 stitches along the other side of the bag bottom. Place a stitch marker. *You now have* 92 stitches.
	Turn the work so that the right side of the bag bottom faces you. Reverse direction this one time only. From here on knit continuous rounds. (See page 173 for information about knitting in the round.)

Marking Rounds

Use a different color stitch marker for the one that marks the beginning of a round.

ROUND 1	*Purl 1, knit to next marker, slip marker; repeat from * to end of round. These purl stitches provide a line for the "lunch bag" folds you will make when you shape the bag after felting.
NEXT ROUNDS	Repeat Round 1 until piece measures 22" (56cm) from the bag bottom.
	Bind off, leaving a 10" (25cm) tail. Thread tail through a yarn needle and draw yarn through the first bound-off stitch, to even the edge. Fasten off and weave tail into wrong side of bag.

KNITTING THE HANDLES

NOTE	The handles are knit in stockinette stitch (knit 1 row, purl 1 row) on straight needles for 10 rows. The cast-on yarn is then pulled out so that you can pick up the first live row of stitches and use Kitchener stitch to create a seamless tube. Make two identical handles.
SET UP	Using a 4 yd (3.6m) length of waste yarn and straight needles, cast on 96 stitches. Cut any extra waste yarn, leaving a 6" (15cm) tail.
ROW 1	Using cc A, knit to end of row. Turn.
ROW 2	Purl to end of row. Turn.
ROWS 3–6	Repeat Rows 1 and 2. At the end of Row 6, cut cc A, leaving a 10" (25cm) tail.
ROW 7	Using cc B, knit to end of row. Turn.
ROW 8	Purl to end of row. Turn.
ROWS 9–10	Repeat Rows 7 and 8. Do not bind off after Row 10.

FINISHING THE HANDLES

NOTE	In this section, you will be creating the tubes that form the handles of the bag. The handles are stabilized by seam binding to keep them from stretching during use. The seam binding is applied before felting, since the two layers of the handles fuse during the felting process.

With right side facing you and working stitch by stitch, pull out the waste yarn cast-on edge, placing the live stitches that form the first row of cc A on the free straight needle. When all the cast-on stitches are removed, the tip of the needle containing the stitches worked in Row 10 and the tip of the needle now containing the stitches worked in Row 1 should be aligned.

Use Kitchener stitch to graft the stitches on the two needles together.
(See page 172 for instructions on how to do Kitchener stitch.)

Thread a yarn needle with 2½ yds (2.25m) of seam binding, and draw the seam binding through the length of the handle. Using sewing thread and needle, baste binding to handle at each end; cut off any excess binding.

Flatten the handle so that the band of cc B is entirely within one side of the handle, with about 1 row of cc A showing at each edge. Using cc A, make a line of running stitches just inside both edges of the handle to hold it flat and properly aligned. These can be basting-length stitches (about ½"/1.25cm long), as long as only small stitches show on the outer faces of the handle. These stitches will disappear into the fabric when the handles are felted.

KNITTING THE I-CORD LOOP AND ROSE FASTENER

Using cc A and the double point needles, cast on 3 stitches. Following the directions on page 171, work a 20" (51cm) long I-cord.

Drawing the yarn from behind, knit the 3 stitches together and fasten off, leaving a 10" (25cm) tail. Pull the tails to the inside at both ends of the I-cord.

Using cc B and the double point needles, cast on 3 stitches. Work a 20" (51cm) long I-cord, and finish in the same manner as for the loop.

tip

Removing Waste Yarn

You can more easily remove the waste yarn if you cut it every few stitches.

Following the directions on page 9, felt the bag, I-cord loop, and both handles at the same time.

After removing as much excess water as possible, shape the bag by folding the sides firmly up, using the purl stitches around the base of the bag as a guide. Fold the sides of the bag lengthwise along the purl stitches that mark the corners. Flatten the bag so that the wide sides face out and the narrow sides fold in, like a typical paper lunch bag (see illustration). Pull the bag firmly as needed to square up all corners. Stuff it lightly with plastic bags or paper towels so that it can dry standing up. Avoid disturbing the folds you've made at the corners and at the sides.

Lay the handles straight to dry, pressing them to flatten as much as possible.

Smooth and stretch the I-cord loop and fastener and let them dry.

SEWING ON THE HANDLES AND LOOP

Following the drawing at right, pin the handles in place, with the contrasting color side of the handle against the right side of the bag. Make sure that the handles are not twisted. Using mc, sew the handles securely to the bag with a decorative X stitch, as shown.

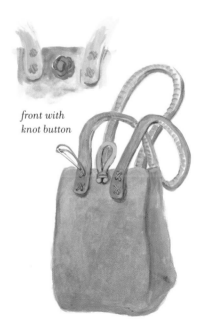

front with knot button

Take the I-cord knitted with cc B for the fastener and tie it in a loose overhand knot at the center. Make a second overhand knot at the same spot, and tuck the ends into the knot so that they don't show. (If the fastener is too large, trim a bit off each end until it is the size you like.) Using matching sewing thread, sew the fastener securely to the bag about 1¼" (3cm) from the top edge at the center. Be sure to stitch through the knot itself, not the loose ends.

Fold the loop in half and attach it securely on the outside of the bag at the center back, adjusting it as needed to fit around the fastener.

Soft-and-Thick Shoulder Bag

Rug yarn makes an especially sturdy, thick fabric for this attractive shoulder bag. It's just the right size for every day needs. You may want to line it to increase its serviceability (see page 25 for instructions).

YARN
Halcyon Yarn Rug Wool, 100% wool, 65 yd (60m)/4 oz (113g) skeins

mc
165 yds (151m) #107 Russet

cc A
25 yds (23m)   #122 Slate Blue

cc B
25 yds (23m)   #154 Teal

cc C
40 yds (37m)   #113 Red-Purple

cc D
15 yds (14m)   #179 Orange

NEEDLES
ONE SET of US #13 (9mm) double point needles, *or size you need to obtain gauge*
ONE circular needle, 24" (60cm) long, *same size as above*

GAUGE, BEFORE FELTING
5 stitches = 2" (5cm), 6 rows = 2" (5cm) in stockinette stitch

NUMBER OF WASH CYCLES TO ACHIEVE SAMPLE SIZE
Three

OTHER SUPPLIES
Stitch marker, yarn needle

ABBREVIATIONS
cc   contrast color
mc   main color

APPROXIMATE MEASUREMENTS

Before Felting
14" (36cm) wide, 12½" (32cm) tall

After Felting
11¼" (29cm) wide, 8½ " (22cm) long

KNITTING THE FLAP

NOTE	For the flap, you will be working back and forth in rows in stockinette stitch, turning at the end of each row.
SET UP	With the circular needle and mc yarn, cast on 36 stitches.
ROWS 1–2	Work each row in stockinette stitch (knit 1 row, turn, purl 1 row, turn).
ROWS 3–10	Continuing in stockinette stitch, follow the color pattern shown in the Shoulder Bag Flap Chart on the facing page. Start with Line 1 at the bottom right. (For advice about two-color knitting, see Fair Isle knitting, page 171.) As you work the chart, continue in stockinette stitch, following the chart from right to left on right-side (knit) rows, and from left to right on wrong-side (purl) rows.
ROWS 11–20	Using mc, work each row in stockinette stitch.

KNITTING THE BAG

SET UP	At the beginning of the next right-side row, cast on another 36 stitches. *You now have* 72 stitches.
ROUND 1	Knit the 36 cast-on stitches, and then continue knitting the 36 flap stitches. Place a stitch marker to indicate the beginning of the round, and join the stitches in a round, taking care that no stitches are twisted around the needle. (For advice about knitting in the round, see page 173.)
ROUNDS 2–10	Knit to the end of each round.
ROUNDS 11–30	Continuing to knit to the end of each round, follow the color pattern shown in the Shoulder Bag Chart on the facing page. Start with Line 1 at the bottom right and work the chart from right to left.
ROUNDS 31–40	Change to mc, and knit to the end of each round.

FINISHING THE BOTTOM

Divide the stitches between two double point needles. Use a third double point needle to cast off all stitches, using the 3-needle cast-off technique (see pages 173–174).

Cut yarns, leaving a 10" (25cm) tail. Thread the yarn through a yarn needle and weave the tail to the inside of the bag. Weave in any other loose ends.

MAKING THE I-CORD HANDLE

SET UP   Using a double point needle and cc C, pick up 4 stitches on the inside at one side top edge, where the flap joins the bag.

Work a 30" (76cm) I-cord, following the directions on page 171.

LAST ROW   Bring yarn around back of work, and knit the 4 stitches together.

Break yarn, leaving a 10" (25cm) tail. Thread the tail through a yarn needle, and sew the end of the I-cord securely to the opposite side of the bag, being careful not to twist the handle.

FELTING AND SHAPING THE BAG

Felt according to the instructions on page 9. Smooth the handbag on a flat surface taking care to make all edges straight and corners square. Smooth the handle, stretching if necessary. Allow the bag to dry completely.

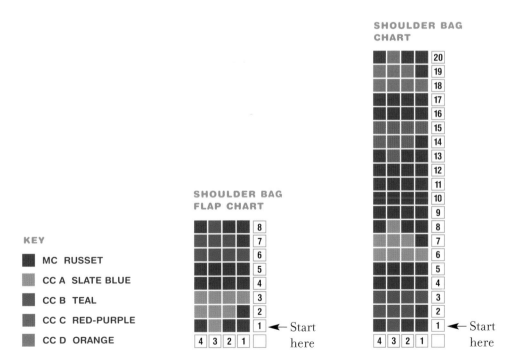

KEY

- ■ MC RUSSET
- ■ CC A SLATE BLUE
- ■ CC B TEAL
- ■ CC C RED-PURPLE
- ■ CC D ORANGE

SHOULDER BAG FLAP CHART

← Start here

SHOULDER BAG CHART

← Start here

Scallops and Beads

Strands of two rich, closely related shades of yarn are held together to knit the body of this bag. The contrasting electric blue and green trim colors not only set off the main color, but provide interesting design features: The green scalloped border is tipped by small beads, and the blue rolled cuff forms a firm edging around the top. The green and blue yarns tend to shrink a bit more during the felting, as well, which adds shape and security at the top of the bag.

YARN

Harrisville Designs Highland Style, 100% wool, worsted weight, 200 yd (183m)/3.5 oz (100g) skeins

mc	130 yds (119m)	Plum
cc A	130 yds (119m)	Magenta

Brown Sheep Lamb's Pride, 85% wool/15% mohair, worsted weight, 190 yd (174m)/4 oz (114g) skeins

cc B	30 yds (27m)	Limeade
cc C	40 yds (36m)	Sapphire

NEEDLES

ONE US #13 (9mm) circular needle, 16" (25cm) long, *or size you need to obtain gauge*

ONE SET of US #13 (9mm) double point needles, *or same size as above*

GAUGE, BEFORE FELTING

5 stitches = 2" (5cm), 6 rows = 2" (5cm) with 2 strands of yarn in stockinette stitch

NUMBER OF WASH CYCLES TO ACHIEVE SAMPLE SIZE

Two

OTHER SUPPLIES

Stitch markers; yarn needle; one bobbin NYMO Size D thread and needle; 10 large, 10 medium, and 10 small beads

ABBREVIATIONS

cc	contrast color
mc	main color

APPROXIMATE MEASUREMENTS

Before felting

15" (38cm) wide, 12" (31cm) tall

After felting

10½" (27cm) wide, 8" (21cm) tall, with cuff rolled down

STARTING FROM THE BASE

NOTE

Work the base by knitting back and forth in rows on the circular needle without joining. After 8 rows, pick up stitches around base and join in the round.

SET UP

Holding one strand of mc and one strand of cc A together, use the circular needle to cast on 30 stitches.

ROWS 1–8

Knit to the end of each row, then turn.

KNITTING THE SIDES

ROUND 1

Knit the 30 stitches. Place a stitch marker.

Pick up and knit 5 stitches along the short end of the base. Place a stitch marker. Pick up and knit 30 stitches along the long side of the base. Place a stitch marker. Pick up and knit 5 stitches along the other short end of the base. Place a stitch marker. (Use a different color stitch marker for the last one, to mark the beginning of the round.) You now have 70 stitches.

ROUNDS 2–12

Knit to end of each round, slipping markers as you come to them.

ROUND 13

*Knit 4, knit 2 together; repeat from * to first stitch marker. Slip marker. Knit 5. Slip second marker. *Knit 4, knit 2 together; repeat from * to third stitch marker. Slip marker. Knit 5. Slip fourth marker. *You now have* 60 stitches.

ROUNDS 14–24

Knit to end of each round, slipping markers as you come to them.

ROUND 25

*Knit 3, knit 2 together; repeat from * to first stitch marker. Slip marker. Knit 5. Slip second marker. *Knit 3, knit 2 together; repeat from * to third stitch marker. Slip marker. Knit 5. Slip fourth marker. *You now have* 50 stitches.

ROUNDS 26–35

Knit to end of each round, slipping markers as you come to them.

ROUNDS 36–41

Follow Triangles Chart (opposite), starting at Line 1 at the bottom right, and repeating the 5-stitch pattern 10 times. Continue to use mc and cc A together for background; use 2 strands of cc B for second color.

ROUND 42

Change to 2 strands of cc C. Knit to end of round.

ROUND 43

Purl to end of round.

Repeat rounds 42–43 three more times.

Bind off, leaving a 10" (25cm) tail. Thread tail through a yarn needle, and draw yarn through first bound-off stitch, to even the edge, then weave tail into *right* side of bag. (The cc C section will roll forward.)

KNITTING THE I-CORD HANDLE

Holding 1 strand of mc and 1 strand of cc A together and using double point needles, pick up and knit 3 stitches on the *inside* at the side in the cc B section of the bag. Use these 3 stitches to knit a 30" (76cm) long I-cord handle (see page 171 for instructions). Cut yarn, leaving a 10" (25cm) tail. Thread tail through a yarn needle, and draw tail through remaining stitches. Use tail to sew end of I-cord securely to inside of bag opposite other end of handle.

FINISHING

Felt the bag, following the instructions on page 9. Then, smooth it on a flat surface, making sure all corners are square and edges even; pin in place, if necessary. Smooth and flatten I-cord handle. Allow to dry completely.

Draw a needle threaded with NYMO thread through bag from inside at one of the points in the cc B section. Thread three beads on the needle, with the largest at the top closest to bag. Using smallest bead as an anchor at bottom, bring thread down and up through beads twice, then fasten it off on inside. Repeat at each of the other points. Take care not to pull thread too tightly, since beads should hang flat on bag.

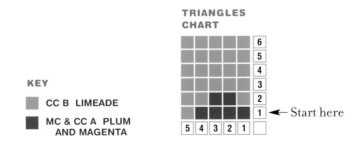

KEY

■ CC B LIMEADE

■ MC & CC A PLUM
    AND MAGENTA

Secret Treasures

This colorful little bag is the perfect size to hold all your special treasures —
or use it to keep your cell phone safe and at hand. The loosely spun merino
yarn creates a soft, thick, but still flexible fabric when felted.

When knitting Fair Isle in felted projects, it is especially important to
keep carried yarns loose, so that the fabric doesn't draw in at those places.

YARN
Morehouse Farm Merino,
3-strand (worsted weight), 140 yd
(128m)/2 oz (57g) skeins

mc	65 yds (59m)	Pumpkin
cc A	25 yds (23m)	Sunflower
cc B	25 yds (23m)	Fuchsia
cc C	20 yds (18m)	Cardinal

NEEDLES
ONE SET US #9 (5.5mm) double
point needles, *or size you need to
obtain gauge*

GAUGE, BEFORE FELTING
9 stitches = 2" (5cm), 12 rows =
2" (5cm) in stockinette stitch

**NUMBER OF WASH CYCLES TO
ACHIEVE SAMPLE SIZE**
Two

OTHER SUPPLIES
Yarn needle

ABBREVIATIONS

cc	contrast color
mc	main color

APPROXIMATE MEASUREMENTS

Before Felting
7" (18cm) wide, 14" (36cm) long

After Felting
4½" (12cm) wide, 7" (18cm) long

KNITTING THE SIDES

SET UP

Using mc and double point needles, cast on 60 stitches. Divide stitches evenly among three needles. Join, being careful not to twist stitches. (For advice about knitting in the round, see page 173.)

ROUNDS 1–46

Work Treasure Bag Chart (opposite), starting with Line 1 at bottom right. The pattern repeats 15 times around. Carry the non-working yarn loosely across the back. (For advice about working with two colors, see Fair Isle knitting, page 171.)

ROUNDS 47–50

Change to mc. Knit to end of each round.

DECREASING AT THE BOTTOM OF THE BAG

ROUND 1

*Knit 4, knit 2 together; repeat from * to end of round. *You now have* 50 stitches.

ROUNDS 2, 4, 6, 8, AND 10

Knit to end of each round.

ROUND 3

*Knit 3, knit 2 together; repeat from * to end of round. *You now have* 40 stitches.

ROUND 5

*Knit 2, knit 2 together; repeat from * to end of round. *You now have* 30 stitches.

ROUND 7

*Knit 1, knit 2 together; repeat from * to end of round. *You now have* 20 stitches.

ROUND 9

*Knit 2 together; repeat from * to end of round. *You now have* 10 stitches.

ROUND 11

*Knit 2 together; repeat from * to end of round. *You now have* 5 stitches.

Don't Pucker Up

Take special care to keep non-working yarn loose when you change needles — a trouble spot, especially for felted items.

KNITTING THE I-CORD DECORATION

Slide the 5 remaining stitches onto one needle. Knit 2 together, knit 2 together, knit 1. *You now have* 3 stitches.

Use these 3 stitches to knit a 1" (2.5cm) long I-cord, following the instructions on page 171.

Bringing the yarn across the back of the work, knit the 3 remaining stitches together.

Cut yarn, leaving a 10" (25cm) long tail. Thread tail through a yarn needle, and draw yarn through remaining stitch. Fasten off. Draw tail up inside the I-cord.

Weave in all remaining loose ends on the inside of the bag.

BRAIDING THE SHOULDER STRAP

Cut two 48" (120cm) lengths each of mc, cc A, and cc B. Make an overhand knot about 1" (2.5cm) from one end. Divide the 6 strands into 3 pairs of same-color yarns; braid the entire length. Finish with an overhand knot about 1" (2.5cm) from the other end.

Use mc threaded in a yarn needle to attach one end of the shoulder strap to each side of the bag on the outside about 1" (2.5cm) from the top edge.

FINISHING

Felt the bag, following the instructions on page 9.

When the bag is felted as desired, smooth it on a flat surface, shaping it so that the design is even. Smooth and stretch the shoulder strap. Allow bag to dry thoroughly. Trim unfinished ends of shoulder strap to even, if necessary.

46
45
44
43
42
41
40
39
38
37
36
35
34
33
32
31
30
29
28
27
26
25
24
23
22
21
20
19
18
17
16
15
14
13
12
11
10
9
8
7
6
5
4
3
2
1 ← Start here

4 3 2 1

KEY

MC PUMPKIN

CC A SUNFLOWER

CC B FUCHSIA

CC C CARDINAL

3 At the Drop of a Hat

A Classic Cloche

Whether you roll the brim up or draw it down, you'll love wearing this easy-to-knit classic. Simple enough for a first-time project, this hat looks dramatically different after felting, so don't worry about its prefelting floppy appearance.

YARN
Brown Sheep Prairie Silks, 10% silk/18% mohair/72% wool, 88 yd (80m)/1.75 oz (50g) skeins

mc   Krona Coffee (PS250)
    Child: 140 yds (126m)
    Adult Small: 160 yds (144m)
    Adult Large: 240 yds (216m)

cc A   Ruble Red (PS400)
    Child: 50 yds (45m)
    Adult Small: 60 yds (54m)
    Adult Large: 70 yds (63m)

cc B   King's Rubies (PS425)
    Child: 50 yds (45m)
    Adult Small: 60 yds (54m)
    Adult Large: 70 yds (63m)

NEEDLES
ONE US #11 (8mm) circular needle, 24" (61cm) long, *or size you need to obtain gauge*
ONE SET double point needles, *same size as above*

SIZES
Child, Adult Small, Adult Large

GAUGE, BEFORE FELTING
6 stitches = 2" (5cm), 8 rows = 2" (5cm) in stockinette stitch

NUMBER OF WASH CYCLES TO ACHIEVE SAMPLE SIZE
Three

OTHER SUPPLIES
Yarn needle, stitch marker

ABBREVIATIONS
cc   contrast color
mc   main color

APPROXIMATE MEASUREMENTS

	Before Felting	After Felting
CHILD	24" (61cm) circumference, 12" (31cm) tall	18" (46cm) circumference, 6" (15cm) tall
ADULT SMALL	28" (71cm) circumference, 13" (33cm) tall	20" (51cm) circumference, 6½" (17cm) tall
ADULT LARGE	32" (81cm) circumference, 15" (38cm) tall	22" (56cm) circumference, 9" (23cm) tall

KNITTING THE BRIM

		CHILD	ADULT SM.	ADULT LG.
SET UP	With mc and circular needle, cast on	78 stitches	90 stitches	102 stitches
	Join, being careful not to twist the stitches. (For advice about knitting in the round, see page 173.)			
FIRST ROUNDS	Knit to end of each round for	16 rounds	16 rounds	20 rounds
CHART ROUNDS	Work Cloche Chart (page 56). Be sure to carry non-working yarn very loosely across back of hat. (For advice about working with two colors, see Fair Isle knitting, page 171.) Begin chart at Line 1 at the bottom right. Repeat the 6-stitch pattern around	13 times	15 times	17 times
	When chart is complete, using mc, continue to knit each round for	6 rounds	10 rounds	14 rounds

DECREASING FOR THE CROWN, ADULT SMALL AND LARGE SIZES ONLY

		CHILD	ADULT SM.	ADULT LG.
NOTE	The larger sizes have more decrease rounds. This section takes you through decreases first for Adult Large and then for Adult Small. Note that the final rounds in this section are for both Adult Large and Adult Small. If you are knitting Child size, skip to the next section. When the hat becomes too narrow to fit comfortably on circular needle, divide stitches evenly among three double point needles and continue to work circularly.			
Large only, ROUND 1	*Knit 2 together, knit 50; repeat from * one more time. *You now have*	——	——	100 stitches
Large only, ROUND 2	Knit to end of round.			

	CHILD	ADULT SM.	ADULT LG.
Large only ROUND 3 — *Knit 8, knit 2 together; repeat to end of round. You now have*	——	——	90 stitches
Adult sizes only, NEXT ROUND — Knit to end of round.			
Adult sizes only, NEXT ROUND — *Knit 7, knit 2 together; repeat from * to end of round. You now have*	——	80 stitches	80 stitches
Adult sizes only, NEXT ROUND — Knit to end of round.			

DECREASING FOR THE CROWN, ALL SIZES

	CHILD	ADULT SM.	ADULT LG.
ROUND 1 — *Knit 6, knit 2 together; repeat from * to end of round, ending	knit 6	——	——
You now have*	70 stitches	70 stitches	70 stitches
ROUNDS 2, 4, 6, 8, 10, 12, AND 14 — Knit to end of each round.			
ROUND 3 — *Knit 5, knit 2 together; repeat from * to end of round. You now have*	60 stitches	60 stitches	60 stitches
ROUND 5 — *Knit 4, knit 2 together; repeat from * to end of round. You now have*	50 stitches	50 stitches	50 stitches
ROUND 7 — *Knit 3, knit 2 together; repeat from * to end of round. You now have*	40 stitches	40 stitches	40 stitches
ROUND 9 — *Knit 2, knit 2 together; repeat from * to end of round. You now have*	30 stitches	30 stitches	30 stitches
ROUND 11 — *Knit 1, knit 2 together; repeat from * to end of round. You now have*	20 stitches	20 stitches	20 stitches
ROUND 13 — *Knit 2 together; repeat from * to end of round. You now have*	10 stitches	10 stitches	10 stitches

	CHILD	ADULT SM.	ADULT LG.
ROUND 15 *Knit 2 together; repeat from * to end of round. *You now have*	5 stitches	5 stitches	5 stitches

Cut yarn, leaving a tail 10" (25cm) long. Thread tail through a yarn needle, and draw yarn through remaining 5 stitches. Fasten off. Weave in all loose ends on the inside of the hat.

FINISHING

Following the instructions on page 9, felt the hat. When the hat has felted as much as is desired, shape the wet crown into a dome. Pay particular attention to the two-color portion of the hat, stretching it as needed. Smooth and roll the brim up, if desired.

The crown should hold its shape without support, but you may wish to dry it over a bowl of the appropriate size so that it doesn't shrink more during the drying period.

CLOCHE CHART

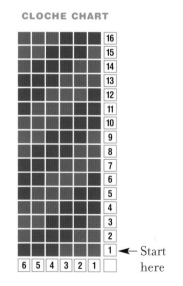

← Start here

KEY

■ MC KRONA COFFEE

■ CC A RUBLE RED

■ CC B KING'S RUBIES

FELTING FRIENDS

On the facing page and on pages 77, 107, 123, and 133, I'd like to indroduce you to some felting artists who have taken the craft into some very creative and inspiring directions.

Cindy Walker

Cindy Walker's home business is run right out of her head and her kitchen. A knitter and pattern writer, Cindy specializes in warm hands and feet with a wide range of hat and slipper patterns, and more recently, handbags. She has also created a sideline of handmade knitting needles and knitting-related humorous cards. The challenge of running her business out of her home is finding a way to separate work from relaxation. The knitting she once did to relax and relieve stress is now the work she does for a living. "I knit for pleasure, too, sometimes," she says, "but I have a separate chair for knitting and writing when it's for work."

Preferring either loosely knitted, lacy styles or the solid, thick weight of felt, with no in-betweens, Cindy tends to knit to a fairly loose gauge, which led her to try felting items that turned out too big. For most felting, she uses a washing machine. "It's just magical," she says. If the washer doesn't work, she sometimes can get the fabric to felt the old-fashioned way, on a washboard. If it still doesn't felt, she's pragmatic about failures. "I love to knit," she says, "so the worst thing that can happen is to knit another."

Cindy double-strands a worsted-weight yarn with a much thinner wool, which she feels increases the effect of agitation; the combination felts beauti-fully. She buys ivory-color wool and dyes everything in her kitchen. As for her patterns, she frequently researches old patterns, including some from the 1940s. "Folks have been felting and making beautiful things since there was wool," she says.

When testing a new pattern, Cindy knits a tiny version first — "preemie sized," she calls it. When she works the pattern up for larger sizes, she uses more math than she'd ever expected. Students often ask her how much money one can make as a home-based fiber artist. "I tell them I'm doing what I love," she laughs, "and when you're doing what you love, the money comes. It really just comes out of the clear blue."

Stripes and Curlicues

What toddler wouldn't love this spiffy hat with felted tassels? And what knitter wouldn't love making it? Although the yarns we used to knit this hip little hat are quite soft, if you're afraid wool might cause delicate baby skin to itch, line the hat with polyester fleece or silk fabric.

YARN
Harrisville Designs Highland Style, 100% wool, worsted weight, 200 yd (183m)/3.5 oz (100g) skeins

mc   Iris
Infant: 40 yds (37m);
Toddler: 45 yds (42m);
Child: 60 yds (55m)

cc A   Topaz
Infant: 30 yds (27m);
Toddler: 35 yds (32m);
Child: 40 yds (37m)

cc B   Violet
Infant: 30 yds (27m);
Toddler: 35 yds (32m);
Child: 40 yds (37m)

cc C   Olive
Infant: 25 yds (23m);
Toddler: 30 yds (27m);
Child: 35 yds (32m)

NEEDLES
ONE SET US #11 (8mm) double point needles, 10" (25cm) long, *or size you need to obtain gauge*

SIZES
Infant, Toddler, Child

GAUGE, BEFORE FELTING
7 stitches = 2" (5cm), 9 rows = 2" (5cm), in stockinette stitch

NUMBER OF WASH CYCLES TO ACHIEVE SAMPLE SIZE
One

OTHER SUPPLIES
Yarn needle, stitch holder

ABBREVIATIONS
cc   contrast color
mc   main color

APPROXIMATE MEASUREMENTS

	Before Felting	After Felting (with brim rolled)
INFANT	18" (46cm) circumference, 12" (31cm) tall	14" (36cm) circumference, 6" (15cm) tall
TODDLER	22" (56cm) circumference, 13" (33cm) tall	15" (38cm) circumference, 7" (18cm) tall
CHILD	24" (61cm) circumference, 14" (36cm) tall	19" (49cm) circumference, 8" (21cm) tall

STARTING FROM THE BRIM

		INFANT	TODDLER	CHILD
SET UP	With mc, cast on	60 stitches	70 stitches	80 stitches
	Distribute the stitches evenly among three needles. Join, being careful not to twist the stitches. For advice about knitting in the round, see page 173. Refer to Stripes Sequence charts on page 63 for guidance throughout the following sections.			
ROUNDS 1–8	Knit to end of each round.			
ROUNDS 9–10	Change to cc A. Knit to end of each round.			
ROUNDS 11–12	Change to mc. Knit to end of each round.			

KNITTING THE SIDES

	INFANT	TODDLER	CHILD
Change to cc A. Knit	7 rounds	8 rounds	9 rounds
Change to cc B. Knit	2 rounds	2 rounds	2 rounds
Change to cc A. Knit	2 rounds	2 rounds	2 rounds
Change to cc B. Knit	7 rounds	8 rounds	9 rounds
Change to cc C. Knit	2 rounds	2 rounds	2 rounds
Change to cc B. Knit	2 rounds	2 rounds	2 rounds
Change to cc C. Knit	7 rounds	8 rounds	9 rounds

DECREASING FOR THE CROWN, CHILD AND TODDLER SIZES

NOTE	Child Size requires 4 extra rounds at the beginning of this section. Toddler Size requires 2 extra rounds at the beginning of this section.

		INFANT	TODDLER	CHILD
Child Size only	Change to mc. *Knit 6, knit 2 together; repeat from * to end of round. *You now have*	—	—	70 stitches
Child Size only	Knit to end of round.			
Child and Toddler Sizes only	With mc, *knit 5, knit 2 together; repeat from * to end of round.	—	60 stitches	60 stitches
Child and Toddler Sizes only	Knit to end of round.			

DECREASING FOR THE CROWN, ALL SIZES

ROUND 1	With cc C, *knit 4, knit 2 together; repeat from * to end of round. *You now have*	50 stitches	50 stitches	50 stitches
ROUNDS 2, 4, 6, AND 8	Knit to end of each round.			
ROUND 3	Change to mc. *Knit 3, knit 2 together; repeat from * to end of round. *You now have*	40 stitches	40 stitches	40 stitches
ROUND 5	Change to cc C. *Knit 2, knit 2 together; repeat from * to end of round. *You now have*	30 stitches	30 stitches	30 stitches
ROUND 7	*Knit 1, knit 2 together; repeat from * to end of round. *You now have*	20 stitches	20 stitches	20 stitches
ROUND 9	*Knit 2 together; repeat from * to end of round. *You now have*	10 stitches	10 stitches	10 stitches

MAKING THE I-CORD CURLICUES

TASSEL 1	With mc, knit 3. Place the remaining 7 stitches on a stitch holder.			
	Make a 12-row I-cord, and fasten off. (See I-cord, page 171, for instructions.)			

TASSEL 2	Place 3 stitches from the stitch holder on an empty needle. With cc A, make another 12-row I-cord, and fasten off.
TASSEL 3	Place 2 stitches from the stitch holder on an empty needle. With cc B, cast on 1 extra stitch. Using cc B, make another 12-row I-cord, and fasten off.
TASSEL 4	Place remaining 2 stitches from the stitch holder on an empty needle. With cc C, cast on 1 extra stitch. Make another 12-row I-cord, and fasten off.

With a yarn needle and mc, tack the curlicues together at their bases to form a solid closure at the top of the hat. Weave in all loose ends on inside of hat.

FINISHING

Felt the hat according to the instructions on page 9. When the hat has felted to the desired size, shape the wet crown into a dome. Smooth and roll up the brim. Smooth and arrange the curlicues. The crown should hold its shape without support, but you may wish to dry it over a bowl of the correct size to keep it from shrinking further. Allow it to dry completely.

Roll Over

If you want a slightly taller crown on the finished hat, don't roll the brim. Simply shape the hat with the lower edge unrolled as it is drying.

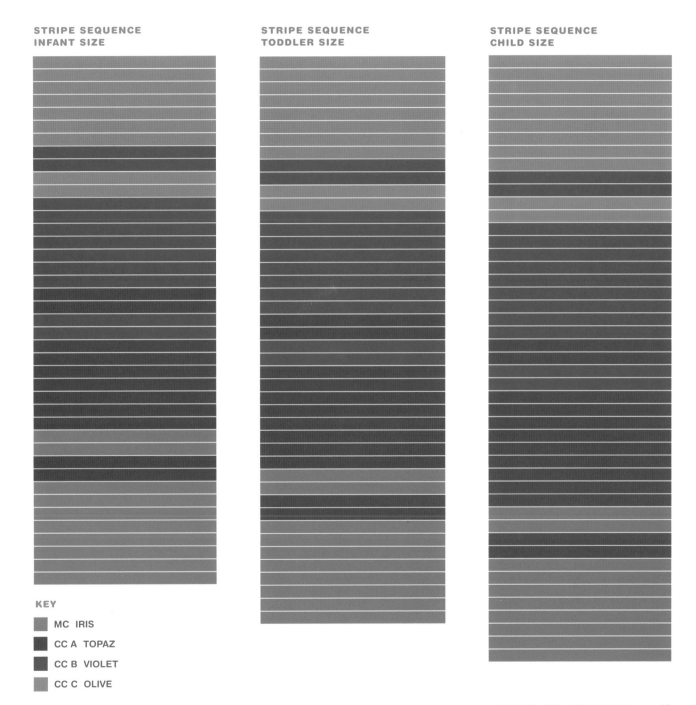

STRIPE SEQUENCE
INFANT SIZE

STRIPE SEQUENCE
TODDLER SIZE

STRIPE SEQUENCE
CHILD SIZE

KEY

MC IRIS

CC A TOPAZ

CC B VIOLET

CC C OLIVE

Peruvian-Style Hat

This ear-flap hat is not only warm, practical, and great-looking, but it is the perfect project for using up odds and ends of leftover yarn. For extra warmth, or to prevent itching, you may wish to line the flaps or the whole hat with polyester fleece or silk fabric.

YARN

Harrisville Designs Highland Style, 100% wool, worsted weight, 200 yd (183m)/3.5 oz (100g) skeins

mc   Teal Blue (#16)
Child: 100 yds (92m);
Adult: 125 yds (114m)

cc A   Iris (#28)
Child: 12 yds (11m);
Adult: 15 yds (14m)

cc B   Violet (#21)
Child: 45 yds (41m);
Adult: 50 yds (46m)

cc C   Poppy (#65)
Child: 40 yds (37m);
Adult: 45 yds (41m)

cc D   Bluegrass (#70)
Child: 20 yds (18m);
Adult: 25 yds (23m)

cc E   Olive (#68)
Child: 24 yds (22m);
Adult: 30 yds (28m)

NEEDLES

ONE US #11 (8mm) circular needle, 16" (40cm) long, *or size you need to obtain gauge*

ONE SET double point needles, 10" (25cm) long, *same size as above*

SIZES

Child, Adult

GAUGE, BEFORE FELTING

7 stitches = 2" (5cm), 9 rows = 2" (5cm) in stockinette stitch

NUMBER OF WASH CYCLES TO ACHIEVE SAMPLE SIZE

Two

OTHER SUPPLIES

Yarn needle, fleece fabric and matching thread (optional)

ABBREVIATIONS

cc   contrast color

mc   main color

APPROXIMATE MEASUREMENTS

	Before Felting	After Felting
CHILD	23" (58cm) circumference, 12" (31cm) tall	18" (46cm) circumference, 7" (18cm) tall (not including earflaps)
ADULT	26" (65cm) circumference, 15" (38cm) tall	20" (51cm) circumference, 9" (23cm) tall (not including earflaps)

KNITTING THE EAR FLAPS

		CHILD	ADULT
NOTE	Instructions are for one flap. Make two identical flaps. Knit flaps back and forth in stockinette stitch (knit 1 row, purl 1 row).		
SET UP	With mc and double point needles, cast on 3 stitches.		
ROW 1	Purl to end of row. Turn.		
ROW 2	*Knit 1 stitch, make 1; repeat from * one more time; knit 1 stitch. (See page 172 for how to "make 1.") Turn. *You now have* 5 stitches.		
ROW 3	Purl to end of row. Turn.		
ROW 4	Knit 1 stitch, make 1, knit to within 1 stitch of end of row, make 1, knit 1. Turn. *You now have* 7 stitches.		
ROW 5	Purl to end of row. Turn.		
NEXT ROWS	Repeat Rows 4 and 5	4 more times	5 more times
	You now have	15 stitches	17 stitches
NEXT ROW	Knit to end of row.		
NEXT ROW	Purl to end of row.		
	At the completion of the first earflap, leave the stitches on the needle, then knit another earflap.		

KNITTING THE SIDES

		CHILD	ADULT
SET UP	Slide the stitches for one of the completed ear flaps onto the circular needle. Using mc and with knit side facing you, knit these earflap stitches. Then, cast on	20 stitches	23 stitches
	With knit side facing you, knit the stitches of the other earflap onto the circular needle. Then, cast on another	20 stitches	23 stitches

	CHILD	ADULT
Join the stitches in a round, being careful not to twist any stitches. (For advice about knitting in the round, see page 173.) *You now have*	70 stitches	80 stitches
ROUNDS 1–31 Work Peruvian-Style Hat Chart on page 69, starting with Line 1 at bottom right. Repeat the pattern around the hat, carrying the non-working yarn very loosely across the back. Place a marker at the beginning of the round. (For advice about working with two colors, see Fair Isle knitting, page 171.)		
NEXT ROUNDS With cc A, knit to end of each round for	8 rounds	10 rounds
NEXT ROUND Change to mc, and knit to end of round.		

DECREASING FOR THE CROWN

	CHILD	ADULT
NOTE The adult size requires 2 extra decrease rounds. When the hat becomes too small to fit comfortably on the circular needle, divide stitches among three double point needles.		
Adult Size only, **EXTRA ROUND** *Knit 6, knit 2 together; repeat from * to end of round. *You now have*	—	70 stitches
Adult Size only, **EXTRA ROUND** Knit to end of round.		
ROUND 1 Change to mc. *Knit 5, knit 2 together; repeat from * to end of round. *You now have*	60 stitches	60 stitches
ROUNDS 2, 4, 6, 8, 10, AND 12 Knit to end of round.		
ROUND 3 *Knit 4, knit 2 together; repeat from * to end of round *You now have*	50 stitches	50 stitches
ROUND 5 *Knit 3, knit 2 together; repeat from * to end of round. *You now have*	40 stitches	40 stitches

		CHILD	ADULT
ROUND 7	*Knit 2, knit 2 together; repeat from * to end of round. *You now have*	30 stitches	30 stitches
ROUND 9	*Knit 1, knit 2 together; repeat from * to end of round. *You now have*	20 stitches	20 stitches
ROUND 11	*Knit 2 together; repeat from * to end of round. *You now have*	10 stitches	10 stitches
ROUND 13	*Knit 2 together; repeat from * to end of round. *You now have*	5 stitches	5 stitches

Cut the yarn, leaving a tail 10" (25cm) long. Thread tail through a yarn needle, draw yarn through remaining stitches, and fasten off. Weave in all loose ends on inside of hat.

FINISHING

Following the instructions on page 9, felt hat. With your hands, shape the wet crown into a dome. Place the wet hat over bowl of the correct size, elevated so that earflaps can hang freely during the drying period. Smooth and stretch earflaps as necessary. Allow hat to dry thoroughly.

MAKING THE TIES

FOR THE EARFLAPS Cut four 25" (64cm) lengths each of cc B, cc C, and cc E. Thread two strands of each color through a yarn needle, and draw the yarn through the end of one earflap until all six ends hang evenly. Divide into three sections by color, then make a braid. Tie the braid securely with cc C about 1" (2.5cm) from the end.

FOR THE TOPPER Cut two 12" (31cm) lengths each of cc B, cc C, and cc E. Attach to the center top at the hat, and braid and finish as for the earflaps.

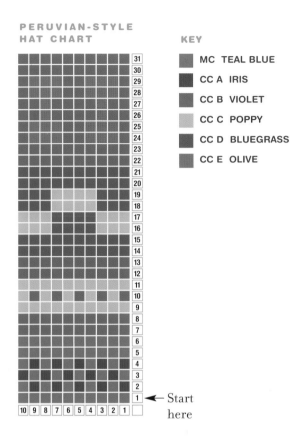

PERUVIAN-STYLE HAT CHART

31
30
29
28
27
26
25
24
23
22
21
20
19
18
17
16
15
14
13
12
11
10
9
8
7
6
5
4
3
2
1 ← Start here

10 9 8 7 6 5 4 3 2 1

KEY

MC TEAL BLUE

CC A IRIS

CC B VIOLET

CC C POPPY

CC D BLUEGRASS

CC E OLIVE

No-Itch Liner

Some people object to wearing wool against their skin because it's too itchy. If this is a problem for you, you can line the ear flaps with a coordinating-color fleece fabric. To line, lay the earflap, right side up on the wrong side of the fleece fabric. Use fabric marking pencil to draw a line around the outside edge. Cut the fleece out a scant ½" (1.25cm) inside the drawn line. Pin the fleece to the earflap on the inside with wrong sides facing, leaving a ½" (1.25cm) border of knitted fabric around the outside edge. You don't need to turn a hem in the fleece, since fleece, like felt, won't ravel. Use matching sewing thread to whipstitch the earflap lining in place.

Fluffy Earmuff Covers

Dress up purchased earmuffs with these easy-to-knit covers. This is an ideal project for using up those bits of yarn left over from your other projects. Once you start, you'll want to make several sets.

YARN

Each set of earmuffs requires 50 yds (46m) each of mc and cc

ORANGE EARMUFFS

mc   Nordic Fiber Arts Vamsegarn, 100% wool, 91 yd (83m)/1.75 oz (50g) skeins, color #V61

cc   GGH Soft-Kid, 70% mohair/25% polymid/5% wool, 153 yd (140m)/1 oz (28g) balls, color #70

PURPLE EARMUFFS

mc   Harrisville Designs Highland Style, 100% wool, worsted weight, 200 yd (183m)/ 3.5 oz. (100g) skeins, Plum (#22)

cc   Berroco Mohair Classic, 78% mohair/13% wool/9% nylon, 93 yd (85m)/1.5 oz (43g) balls, color #1109

RED EARMUFFS

mc   Brown Sheep Lamb's Pride, 85% wool/15% mohair, worsted weight, 190 yd (174m)/4 oz (114g) skeins, Red Baron (#M81)

cc   Classic Elite La Gran Mohair, 74% mohair/13% wool/13% nylon, bulky weight, 90 yd (81m)/1.5 oz (43g) balls, #6541

NEEDLES

ONE SET US #11 (8mm) double point needles, *or size you need to obtain gauge*

GAUGE, BEFORE FELTING

7 stitches = 2" (5cm), 9 rows = 2" (5cm) in stockinette stitch

NUMBER OF WASH CYCLES TO ACHIEVE SAMPLE SIZE

Two

OTHER SUPPLIES

Yarn needle, purchased earmuffs

ABBREVIATIONS

cc   contrast color

mc   main color

APPROXIMATE MEASUREMENTS

Before Felting

4½" (11 cm) diameter

After Felting

3½" (9 cm) diameter

NOTE	Instructions given are for one earmuff cover. Make two.
	Hold 1 strand of worsted yarn and one strand of either mohair or blending filament together throughout.
SET UP	Cast on 30 stitches. Distribute stitches evenly among 3 double point needles. Join, being careful not to twist the stitches. (See page 173 for advice about knitting in the round.)
ROUNDS 1–2	Knit to end of each round.
ROUND 3	*Knit 4, increase 1 by knitting into the front and then into the back of the next stitch; repeat from * to end of round. *You now have* 36 stitches. (For an illustration of this kind of increase, see page 172.)
ROUNDS 4–7	Knit to end of each round.
ROUND 8	*Knit 4, knit 2 together; repeat from * to end of round. *You now have* 30 stitches.
ROUND 9	Knit to end of round.
ROUND 10	*Knit 3, knit 2 together; repeat from * to end of round. *You now have* 24 stitches.
ROUND 11	Knit to end of round.
ROUND 12	*Knit 2, knit 2 together; repeat from * to end of round. *You now have* 18 stitches.
ROUND 13	Knit to end of round.
ROUND 14	*Knit 1, knit 2 together; repeat from * to end of round. *You now have* 12 stitches.
ROUND 15	Knit to end of round.
ROUND 16	*Knit 2 together; repeat from * to end of round. *You now have* 6 stitches.

Cut yarn, leaving a 10" (25cm) tail. With a yarn needle, draw the tail through the remaining stitches. Weave in all loose ends on the inside of the work.

FINISHING

Felt both earmuff covers at the same time, according to the directions on page 9.

While the earmuff covers are still wet, stretch them over the purchased earmuffs. You can remove the original covering, or leave it in place for extra padding.

Allow the earmuff covers to dry on the forms. If desired, brush the dry covers to increase their fuzziness.

NOTE   If the felted earmuff covers are loose, tighten them by sewing a line of gathering stitches along the inside edges and fasten off.

Here's a Real Earful

These earmuff covers are so easy and so much fun to knit that you may enjoy trying some variations. Let the following suggestions fire your creativity:

- Knit one green cover and one red one, for "stop-and-go" earmuffs.
- Make striped earmuff covers by changing colors every round, or every other round. You can use just two different colors, or go for a rainbow of shades.
- If you have leftover luxury yarn, such as cashmere, from another project, consider making the ultimate covering using cashmere.
- Ornament your earmuff covers with needle felting (see page 147 for instructions).

Slipstitch Headband

This color pattern looks like you are using two yarn colors across each row in Fair Isle style, but you aren't! Instead, you work the design of this one-size-fits-all ear warmer with an easy slipstitch technique.

YARN
Nordic Fiber Arts Vamsegarn, 100% wool, 91yd (83m)/ 1.75 oz (50g) skeins

Green and Orange (left)

mc	45 yds (41m)	color #V86
cc	25 yds (23m)	color #V61

Blue and Gold (right)

mc	45 yds (41m)	color #V37
cc	25 yds (23m)	color #V46

NEEDLES
One US #11 (8mm), 16" (40cm) circular needle, *or size you need to obtain gauge*

SIZE
One size fits all

GAUGE, BEFORE FELTING
6 stitches = 2" (5cm), 8 rows = 2" (5cm) in stockinette stitch

NUMBER OF WASH CYCLES TO ACHIEVE SAMPLE SIZE
One

OTHER SUPPLIES
Yarn needle, Velcro closure, matching sewing thread and needle, coordinating fleece fabric (optional), fabric marker

ABBREVIATIONS

cc	contrast color
mc	main color

APPROXIMATE MEASUREMENTS

Before Felting	After Felting
4½" (11cm) wide, 27" (69cm) long	3" (8cm) wide, 25" (64cm) long

NOTE	Always hold yarn on wrong side of work when slipping stitches. All stitches should be slipped purlwise.
SET UP	With mc, cast on 81 stitches.
ROW 1	Purl to end of row. Turn.
ROW 2	Knit to end of row. Turn.
ROW 3	Purl to end of row. Turn. Do not cut mc.
ROW 4	Change to cc. Slip 1 stitch, *knit 3, slip 1; repeat from * to end of row.
ROW 5	*Slip 1, purl 3; repeat from * to last stitch; slip 1. Do not cut cc.
ROW 6	Change to mc. Knit to end of row.
ROW 7	Purl to end of row.
ROW 8	Change to cc. Slip 3, *knit 3, slip 1; repeat from * to last 3 stitches, slip 3.
ROW 9	Slip 3, *purl 3, slip 1; repeat from * to last 3 stitches, slip 3.
ROW 10	Change to mc. Knit to end of row.
ROW 11	Purl to end of row.
ROWS 12–19	Repeat Rows 4–11.
	Bind off.

Wider. . . and Warmer

If you prefer a wider ear warmer, work 8 more rows of the pattern before binding off.

Felt ear warmer, following instructions on page 9. Smooth it flat, and allow it to dry thoroughly. Using a yarn needle, hand-sew one piece of the Velcro closure to each end of the ear warmer. If you mind the itchiness of wool, line it with fleece, *before stitching on the Velcro closure.* Lay ear warmer right-side up on wrong side of coordinating fleece fabric. Use fabric marker to draw around outside edge. Cut fleece a scant ½" (1.25cm) inside drawn line. Whipstitch lining in place on inside of ear warmer.

Beverly Galeskas

SEATTLE, WASHINGTON

ev Galeskas is the founder and driving force behind Washington State-based Fiber Trends, but she didn't learn to knit until age 30. "It's never too late to start," she encourages. Bev's business as a pattern writer and designer started completely by accident. "I was teaching a local class on knitting and felting," she says, "and basically just wanted to build a better mousetrap than the patterns that were out there."

Her felted creations include stuffed animals, such as teddy bears, stuffed sheep, and a koala she's particularly proud of. She's created patterns for every kind of clothing and accessory, but her most successful current design is a felted clog with a double-thick felted sole. She uses several plain worsted yarns in her work, including Brown Sheep yarns and New Zealand wools like Woolpak, which she says felts particularly well.

As a starting point for her designs, Bev likes to study the structure of finished items, such as shoes or stuffed animals. "If the shape can be knit, then it can be knit and felted." A collector of old needlework books, she says, "Every great idea we have today has been tried by other knitters in the past. We're not inventing the wheel." For example, she tells of finding a knitted felt hat in a 1930s magazine. "Their tech-

niques were slightly different, but it was obvious that they knew as much about it as I do."

Her best advice for new knitters is to look at your knitting. "If you can discover what is happening," she advises, "and how the stitches are formed, each new project gets easier. Don't be afraid of mistakes. As soon as you get out of your own way, your hands learn how and you can do anything you want." Bev is the author of *Felted Knits*, a book of knitted felt projects.

Double-Cuff Mittens

Pretty and practical, these double-cuff mittens will keep your hands warm no matter how cold it is outside. The unfelted inside cuff allows for a snug fit and extra warmth. Use same-color yarn for the cuffs, or try a complementary hue.

YARN
Harrisville Designs Highland Style, 100% wool, worsted weight, 200 yd (183m)/3.5 oz (100g) skeins
From left to right: Cornflower (27), Aster (34), Seagreen (12)
Medium: 200 yds (180m)
Large: 220 yds (198m)

NEEDLES
ONE SET US #11 (8mm) double point needles, *or size you need to obtain gauge*
ONE SET US #4 (3.5mm) double point needles, *same size as above*

WOMEN'S SIZES
Medium and large

GAUGE, BEFORE FELTING
7 stitches = 2" (5cm); 9 rows = 2" (5cm), in stockinette stitch on larger needles

NUMBER OF WASH CYCLES TO ACHIEVE SAMPLE SIZE
Two

OTHER SUPPLIES
Yarn needle, stitch markers, stitch holder, matching sewing thread and needle

APPROXIMATE MEASUREMENTS

	Before Felting	After Felting
MEDIUM	5½" (14cm) wide, 14" (35cm) long	4½" (12cm) wide, 9" (23cm) long
LARGE	5½" (14cm) wide, 16" (40cm) long	4½" (12cm) wide, 9¾" (25cm) long

KNITTING THE BOTTOM OF THE HAND

		MEDIUM	LARGE
	Instructions are for one mitten. Make 2 identical mittens.		
SET UP	Using the larger needles, cast on	40 stitches	40 stitches
	Divide the stitches among three double point needles as follows:		
	Needle 1:	12 stitches	12 stitches
	Needle 2:	16 stitches	16 stitches
	Needle 3:	12 stitches	12 stitches
	Join the stitches, taking care that no stitches are twisted around the needles. (For information about knitting in the round, see page 173.)		
ROUNDS 1–20	Knit to end of round.		

MAKING THE GUSSET

		MEDIUM	LARGE
NOTE	To increase in this section, use the technique known as "make 1" (see page 172).		
ROUND 1	Make 1, knit 1, make 1. Place a stitch marker on the needle. Knit to end of round. *You will have* 3 stitches before the stitch marker on Needle 1. *You now have*	42 stitches	42 stitches
ROUNDS 2, 4, 6, 8, 10, AND 12	Knit to end of each round.		
ROUNDS 3, 5, 7, 9, AND 11	Make 1, knit to marker, make 1, slip marker, knit to end of round. After Round 11, you have 13 stitches before the stitch marker on Needle 1. *You now have*	52 stitches	52 stitches

KNITTING THE TOP OF THE HAND

		MEDIUM	LARGE
SET UP	Place the 13 stitches before the stitch marker onto a stitch holder. Remove the stitch marker. Cast on 1 stitch over the opening. *You now have*	40 stitches	40 stitches

	MEDIUM	LARGE
Knit to end of round for	20 rounds	25 rounds

DECREASING FOR THE TOP OF THE FINGERTIPS

		MEDIUM	LARGE
ROUND 1	*Knit 6, knit 2 together; repeat from * to end of round. *You now have*	35 stitches	35 stitches
ROUNDS 2, 4, 6, 8, 10, AND 12	Knit to end of each round.		
ROUND 3	*Knit 5, knit 2 together; repeat from * to end of round. *You now have*	30 stitches	30 stitches
ROUND 5	*Knit 4, knit 2 together; repeat from * to end of round. *You now have*	25 stitches	25 stitches
ROUND 7	*Knit 3, knit 2 together; repeat from * to end of round. *You now have*	20 stitches	20 stitches
ROUND 9	*Knit 2, knit 2 together; repeat from * to end of round. *You now have*	15 stitches	15 stitches
ROUND 11	*Knit 1, knit 2 together; repeat from * to end of round. *You now have*	10 stitches	10 stitches
ROUND 13	*Knit 2 together; repeat from * to end of round. *You now have*	5 stitches	5 stitches

Cut the yarn, leaving a 12" (31cm) tail. Thread the tail through a yarn needle, and draw yarn through the remaining 5 stitches. Fasten off. Weave in the tail on the inside of the mitten.

On Track

To help you keep track of where you are in the round when knitting on double point needles, place a small safety pin on the knitted fabric at the beginning of Needle 1.

KNITTING THE THUMB

		MEDIUM	LARGE
SET UP	Place the 13 stitches from the stitch holder on three of the larger double point needles as follows:		
	Needle 1:	1 stitch	1 stitch
	Needle 2:	6 stitches	6 stitches
	Needle 3:	6 stitches	6 stitches
	Using Needle 1, pick up and knit 5 stitches across the gap. (For an illustration of how to pick up stitches, see page 173.) *You now have* 18 stitches in all. (Needle 1 now has 6 stitches.)		
ROUNDS 1–9	Knit to end of each round.		
ROUND 10	*Knit 1, knit 2 together; repeat from * to end of round. *You now have*	12 stitches	12 stitches
ROUND 11	Knit to end of round.		
ROUND 12	*Knit 2 together; repeat from * to end of round. *You now have*	6 stitches	6 stitches
	Cut the yarn, leaving a 12" (31cm) tail. Thread the tail through a yarn needle, and draw yarn through the remaining 6 stitches. Fasten off. Weave in the tail on the inside of the thumb.		

FINISHING THE FELTED OUTER MITTENS

Weave in any remaining loose ends on the inside of the mittens. Then, felt both mittens at the same time, following the instructions on page 9. When the mittens are felted to desired size, stretch and smooth them as necessary, taking care to make them the same size. Make sure the lower edges are straight.

		MEDIUM	LARGE
NOTE	Instructions are for 1 cuff. Make 2.		
	Using the smaller double point needles, cast on	40 stitches	40 stitches
	Divide the stitches as follows:		
	Needle 1:	12 stitches	12 stitches
	Needle 2:	16 stitches	16 stitches
	Needle 3:	12 stitches	12 stitches
	Join the stitches, taking care that no stitches are twisted around the needles. (For information about knitting in the round, see page 173.)		
ROUNDS 1–20	*Knit 2, purl 2; repeat from * to end of round.		
	Bind off loosely. Weave in all loose tails.		

Turn the mitten inside out. With the cast-on edge of the ribbed cuff toward the bottom of the mitten, stretch the ribbed cuff so that you can slide it over the mitten, with wrong sides facing. Align so that the bound-off edge of the ribbed cuff is just below the beginning of the thumb gusset. The lower (cast-on) edge of the ribbed cuff should not extend beyond the bottom of the mitten.

With matching thread, whipstitch the ribbed cuff in place by sewing the *upper edge* to the inside of the mitten, leaving the lower edge at the bottom of the mitten unsewn. Do not allow your stitches to show on the outside of the mitten. Turn mitten right side out.

Touch-of-Fur Scarf

Here's a scarf that's as much fun to wear as it is to knit. The "fur" that separates the color bands is knit together with the main-color yarn. To maintain some drape, you'll probably want to felt this more lightly than some of the other projects in the book.

YARN
Harrisville Designs Highland Style, 100% wool, worsted weight, 200 yd (183m)/3.5 oz (100g) skeins

mc   215 yds (194m)
      Bermuda Blue (17)

cc A   50 yds (46m)   Iris (28)

cc B   50 yds (46m)   Melon (66)

cc C   35 yds (25m)   Peacock (13)

Firenze (from Halcyon Yarn), 30% wool/30% acrylic/40% nylon, 55 yd (50m)/1.78 oz (50g) balls

cc D   1 ball color #13

NEEDLES
ONE PAIR US #11 (8mm) needles, *or size you need to obtain gauge*

GAUGE, BEFORE FELTING
6 stitches = 2" (5cm),
8 rows = 2" (5cm) in stockinette stitch

NUMBER OF WASH CYCLES TO ACHIEVE SAMPLE SIZE
Two

OTHER SUPPLIES
Yarn needle

ABBREVIATIONS
cc   contrast color

mc   main color

APPROXIMATE MEASUREMENTS

Before Felting

9" (23cm) wide, 90" (218cm) long

After Felting

5¾" (15cm) wide, 57½" (144cm) long

NOTE	The entire scarf is worked in stockinette stitch. Each band of color is separated by 2 rows of mc and cc D worked together. Note that the bands of plain mc contain 12 rows, and the bands of cc A, cc B, and cc C contain 10 rows.
SET UP	Using mc, cast on 27 stitches.
ROW 1	Holding one strand of mc and one strand of cc D together, knit to end of row.
ROW 2	Purl to end of row. Cut cc D.
ROW 3	Using mc only, knit to end of row.
ROW 4	Purl to end of row.
ROW 5	Knit to end of row.
ROW 6	Purl to end of row.
ROWS 7–18	Repeat Rows 5 and 6. You have worked 16 rows of mc.
ROWS 19–20	Using mc and cc D, repeat Rows 5 and 6. Cut cc D.
ROWS 21–30	Using cc A, repeat Rows 5 and 6. You have worked 10 rows of cc A.
ROWS 31–32	Using mc and cc D, repeat Rows 5 and 6. Cut cc D.
ROWS 33–44	Using mc only, repeat Rows 5 and 6. You have worked 12 rows of mc.
ROWS 45–46	Using mc and cc D, repeat Rows 5 and 6. Cut cc D.
ROWS 47–56	Using cc B, repeat Rows 5 and 6. You have worked 10 rows of cc B.
ROWS 57–58	Using mc and cc D, repeat Rows 5 and 6. Cut cc D.
ROWS 59–70	Using mc only, repeat Rows 5 and 6. You have worked 12 rows of mc.
ROWS 71–72	Using mc and cc D, repeat Rows 5 and 6. Cut cc D.
ROWS 73–82	Using cc C, repeat Rows 5 and 6. You have worked 10 rows of cc C.
ROWS 83–84	Using mc and cc D, repeat Rows 5 and 6. Cut cc D.
ROWS 85–96	Using mc only, repeat Rows 5 and 6. You have worked 12 rows of mc.

ROWS 97–98	Using mc and cc D, repeat Rows 5 and 6. Cut cc D.
ROWS 99–176	Following the same color sequence, repeat Rows 21–98.
ROWS 177–186	Using cc B, repeat Rows 5 and 6. You have worked 10 rows of cc B.
ROWS 187–188	Using mc and cc D, repeat Rows 5 and 6. Cut cc D.
ROWS 189–200	Using mc only, repeat Rows 5 and 6. You have worked 12 rows of mc.
ROWS 201–202	Using mc and cc D, repeat Rows 5 and 6. Cut cc D.
ROWS 203–212	Using cc A, repeat Rows 5 and 6. You have worked 10 rows of cc A.
ROWS 213–214	Using mc and cc D, repeat Rows 5 and 6. Cut cc D.
ROWS 215–226	Using mc only, repeat Rows 5 and 6. You have worked 12 rows of mc.
ROWS 227–228	Using mc and cc D, repeat Rows 5 and 6. Cut cc D.
ROWS 229–238	Using cc C, repeat Rows 5 and 6. You have worked 10 rows of cc C.
ROWS 239–240	Using mc and cc D, repeat Rows 5 and 6. Cut cc D.
ROWS 241–252	Using mc only, repeat Rows 5 and 6. You have worked 12 rows of mc.
ROWS 253–254	Using mc and cc D, repeat Rows 5 and 6. Cut cc D.
ROWS 255–292	Following the same color sequence, repeat Rows 177–214. You have worked 10 rows of cc B, 2 rows of mc and cc D, 12 rows of mc, 2 rows of mc and cc D, 10 rows of cc A, and 2 rows of mc and cc D.
ROWS 293–308	Using mc only, repeat Rows 5 and 6. You have worked 16 rows of mc.
ROWS 309–310	Using mc and cc D, repeat Rows 5 and 6.
	Bind off, leaving 10" (25 cm) tails. Thread the tails through a yarn needle, and weave them in on the wrong side of the piece.

FINISHING

Felt the scarf, following the instructions on page 9. Lay the scarf out to dry on a flat surface. Smooth it carefully and be sure that the edges are straight and all corners are square.

Getting on Your Feet

Bunny Hoppers

Even first-time knitters can whip up these adorable bunnies in a flash. The entire slipper is knit in garter stitch (knit every row) on straight needles. Designed to fit a toddler, the slippers can be made larger or smaller by knitting more or fewer rows, respectively, before decreasing for the toe. You can also adjust the finished size by felting (agitating) more or less.

YARN

mc Brown Sheep Lamb's Pride, 85% wool/15% mohair, worsted weight, 190 yd (174m)/4 oz (114g) per skein
120 yds (108m) White Frost (M11) or Deep Charcoal (M06)

cc Halcyon Victorian Brushed Mohair, 70% mohair/24% wool/6% nylon, 145 yd (130m)/2 oz (57g) mini skeins
120 yds (108m) #103 (white) or #134 (black)

NEEDLES
ONE PAIR US #11 (8mm) straight needles, *or size you need to obtain gauge*

SIZE
Toddler

GAUGE, BEFORE FELTING
5½ stitches = 2" (5cm), 8 rows = 2" (5cm) in garter stitch with one strand mc and one strand cc

NUMBER OF WASH CYCLES TO ACHIEVE SAMPLE SIZE
Black: Two
White: Four

OTHER SUPPLIES
Yarn needle, 3" (7.5cm) square of sturdy cardboard, matching sewing thread and needle, bright pink and black crewel embroidery yarn, white quilting thread

ABBREVIATIONS
cc contrast color
mc main color

APPROXIMATE MEASUREMENTS

Before Felting

8½" (22cm) long, 11" (28cm) wide

After Felting

5½" (14cm) long, 2½" (7cm) high

KNITTING FROM THE HEEL

NOTE	Instructions for left and right slippers are identical. Make two. Hold one strand of mc and one strand of cc together throughout the entire project.
SET UP	Cast on 30 stitches.
ROW 1	Knit to end of row. Turn.
NEXT ROWS	Knit to the end of each row until piece measures 6" (15cm) (about 14 garter stitch ridges on the right side).

DECREASING FOR THE TOE

ROW 1	*Knit 4, knit 2 together; repeat from * to end of row. *You now have* 25 stitches.
ROWS 2, 4, 6, AND 8	Knit to end of each row.
ROW 3	*Knit 3, knit 2 together; repeat from * to end of row. *You now have* 20 stitches.
ROW 5	*Knit 2, knit 2 together; repeat from * to end of row. *You now have* 15 stitches.
ROW 7	*Knit 1, knit 2 together; repeat from * to end of row. *You now have* 10 stitches.
ROW 9	*Knit 2 together; repeat from * to end of row. *You now have* 5 stitches.
	Cut yarn, leaving a 10" (25cm) tail. Thread tail through a yarn needle, and draw yarn through the 5 stitches remaining on the needle. Do not cut tail.

KNITTING THE EARS

NOTE	Make four identical ears.
SET UP	Using a strand of mc and a strand of cc together, cast on 6 stitches.
ROW 1	Knit to end of row.
ROW 2	Purl to end of row.
	Repeat Rows 1 and 2 (stockinette stitch) until piece measures 4" (10cm) from the cast-on edge. Stop knitting at the completion of a purl row.

Feeling in the Pink

If you wish, add a little touch of color to the white bunny by substituting a strand of pale pink mohair for the white mohair in the ears and tail.

DECREASE ROW 1	*Knit 2 together; repeat from * to end of row. *You now have* 3 stitches.
DECREASE ROW 2	Purl to end of row.
DECREASE ROW 3	Knit 3 together.

Cut yarn, leaving a 6" (15cm) tail. Thread tail through a yarn needle, and draw yarn through the remaining stitch. Weave in the tail. Do not sew ears to slippers.

SEWING THE SLIPPERS TOGETHER

NOTE

Bunny Hoppers are sewn together in the same manner as the Checkerboard Slippers. Refer to the illustrations on page 106 for further help as you follow these instructions.

Hold the slipper toe edges together with right sides out. Using the yarn tail at the end of the toe, whipstitch the seam for about 4" (10cm). Fasten off and weave the end into the wrong side of the fabric. Then, with right sides still out, hold the slipper heel edges together, and sew along the upper edge for about 2" (5cm). Bring the center bottom of the slipper up to meet the heel seam. Flatten the sides and whipstitch them as shown. See illustration, page 106.)

FINISHING

Felt both slippers and the four ears at the same time, according to the directions on page 9. When the desired degree of felting is reached, arrange the slippers on a flat surface to dry. Flatten the slipper bottoms and smooth the toes so that they are uniformly round. Shape and smooth the ears, but don't worry about making them lay completely flat. They have a natural tendency to curl inward, which makes them look more natural. Allow slippers and ears to dry thoroughly.

MAKING THE POMPOM BUNNY TAIL

Using one strand of mc and one strand of cc, wrap the yarns 20 times around the 3" (7.5 cm) cardboard square. Cut the yarn at each side of the cardboard (see illustration, right), and gently slide the loops off the cardboard.

Wrap a 36" (1m) length of mc once around the center of the loops. Tighten the yarn, and tie it off in a secure knot.

Cut all of the loops and shake the pompom open. Holding the pompom by the long tail, trim the ends so that the ball is uniformly round and about 1" (2.5 cm) in diameter.

Thread tails in a yarn needle, and sew the pompom to the back of the heel, over the heel seam. Stitch through the whole pompom several times to anchor it well. Knot the tail on the inside of the slipper, and weave in the ends.

FINISHING THE EARS AND FEATURES

Fold each ear in half lengthwise. Using matching sewing thread, tack the outside edges together at the bottom (straight) edge. Sew the ears to the slippers about 1" (2.5 cm) from the center of the toe. To help them hold their shape, tack the ears together and to the body of the slipper. (See illustration, opposite.)

Using the crewel embroidery thread, make French knots to embroider eyes. Use bright pink embroidery thread and satin stitch to embroider a nose.

Using quilting thread, make 2 or 3 tiny stitches to fasten the whiskers in place. Leave a 2" (5cm) tail before the stitches, and the same length tail at the end.

If you wish to make the slippers slip-proof, attach fake suede soles to bottoms (see page 25).

Fuzz Up

For added fuzziness, brush the finished slippers with a hair brush or pet comb.

ATTACHING THE EARS

At base (straight edge) of ear, bring corners together and stitch.

Fasten ears to the slipper at the back, to help them stand up.

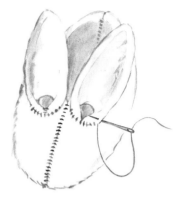

Place additional stitching along front for extra security.

EMBROIDERING THE FEATURES

With crewel yarn, satin stitch a nose; use French knots for eyes.

Make tiny stitches with quilting thread, leaving tails uncut for whiskers.

Fuzzy Toddler Slippers

Soft, cozy, furry — what more could a toddler want? Don't be put off from doing this project because it uses a knitting technique known as "turning the heel." It's really not hard when you follow the directions closely, and you'll be amazed at how quickly and easily these adorable slippers knit up.

YARN

mc   Brown Sheep Lamb's Pride, 85% wool/15% mohair, worsted weight, 190 yd (174m)/4 oz (114g) skeins

125 yds (114m) Lotus Pink (#M38)

cc   Classic Elite La Gran Mohair, 76.5% mohair/17.5% wool/6% nylon, 90 yd (82m)/1.5 oz (43g) balls

125 yds (114m) #6516 (white)

NEEDLES

ONE SET US #11 (8mm) double point needles, *or size you need to obtain gauge*

SIZE

Toddler

GAUGE, BEFORE FELTING

5½ stitches = 2" (5cm), 8 rows = 2" (5cm), using 1 strand each of mc and cc in stockinette stitch

NUMBER OF WASH CYCLES TO ACHIEVE SAMPLE SIZE

Two

OTHER SUPPLIES

Yarn needle; 24"(60cm) of matching ribbon, ⅜" (1cm) wide; matching sewing thread and needle

ABBREVIATIONS

cc   contrast color

mc   main color

APPROXIMATE MEASUREMENTS

Before Felting

8" (20cm) long, 5" (13cm) high

After Felting

6" (15cm) long, 3½" (9cm) high

KNITTING THE ANKLE

NOTE	Work one strand of mc and one strand of cc together throughout the slippers. Left and right slippers are the same; knit two identical slippers.
SET UP	Holding one strand of mc and one strand of cc together, cast on 24 stitches.
	Divide the stitches evenly among three double point needles, 8 stitches per needle. Being careful not to twist the stitches, join the stitches into a round (for information on knitting in the round, see page 173). The first needle is Needle 1; the middle needle is Needle 2; the last needle is Needle 3.
ROUNDS 1 AND 2	Knit to end of each round.

KNITTING THE HEEL FLAP

SET UP	Needle 1: Knit 6 stitches from Needle 1. Slide the remaining 2 stitches from this needle onto Needle 2.
	Needle 3: Slide 6 stitches from Needle 3 onto Needle 1. Slide the remaining 2 stitches from this needle onto Needle 2.
NOTE	*You now have* 12 stitches on each of two needles. In the remainder of this section, you will work on 12 heel stitches, which are on Needle 1. You will return to the other stitches after you turn the heel.
	Work back and forth on the heel stitches in stockinette stitch (knit one row, purl one row).
ROW 1 (WRONG SIDE)	Slip 1, purl to end of row. Turn.
ROW 2	Slip 1, knit to end of row. Turn.
ROWS 3–9	Repeat Rows 1 and 2, ending at the completion of a purl row.

TURNING THE HEEL

ROW 1	Slip 1, knit 5, knit 2 together, knit 1, turn; 3 stitches remain unworked on the needle.

ROW 2	Slip 1, purl 1, purl 2 together, purl 1, turn; 3 stitches remain unworked.
ROW 3	Slip 1, knit 2, knit 2 together, knit 1, turn; 1 stitch remains unworked.
ROW 4	Slip 1, purl 3, purl 2 together, purl 1, turn; 1 stitch remains unworked.
ROW 5	Slip 1, knit 4, knit 2 together, turn. You have worked all stitches at this end of the row.
ROW 6	Slip 1, purl 4, purl 2 together, turn. You have worked all stitches at this end of the row, and *you now have* 6 stitches.

KNITTING THE GUSSET

SET UP	Using the needle with the 6 heel stitches, slip 1, knit 2. The needle that holds these 3 stitches is now Needle 3.
	Needle 1: With a new needle, knit the remaining 3 heel stitches. Pick up and knit 8 stitches along the side of the heel flap.
	Needle 2: This needle contains the 12 stitches you left behind before knitting the heel flap. Knit to the end of this needle.
	Needle 3: Pick up and knit 8 stitches along the other side of the heel flap. Knit the remaining 3 stitches onto this needle.
	You now have 34 stitches in all, divided as follows: Needle 1: 11 stitches Needle 2: 12 stitches Needle 3: 11 stitches
ROUND 1	Knit to end of round.
ROUND 2	Needle 1: Knit to the last 2 stitches, knit 2 together. Needle 2: Knit to end of needle. Needle 3: Knit 2 together, knit to end of needle. *You now have* 32 stitches.
ROUND 3	Knit to end of round.
ROUND 4	Repeat Round 2. *You now have* 30 stitches.

ROUND 5	Knit to end of round.
ROUND 6	Repeat Round 2. *You now have* 28 stitches.
ROUND 7	Knit to end of round.
ROUND 8	Repeat Round 2. *You now have* 26 stitches.
ROUND 9	Knit to end of round.
ROUND 10	Repeat Round 2. *You now have* 24 stitches.

KNITTING THE FOOT

SET UP	Redistribute the stitches evenly among the three needles (8 stitches per needle).
ROUNDS 1–16	Knit to the end of each round.
NOTE	If you wish to make a larger size, knit 4 to 6 more rounds before decreasing for the toe.

DECREASING FOR THE TOE

ROUND 1	*Knit 2, knit 2 together; repeat from * to end of round. *You now have* 18 stitches.
ROUND 2	Knit to end of round.
ROUND 3	*Knit 1, knit 2 together; repeat from * to end of round. *You now have* 12 stitches.
ROUND 4	Knit to end of round.
ROUND 5	*Knit 2 together; repeat from * to end of round. *You now have* 6 stitches.
	Cut yarn, leaving a 10" (25cm) tail. Thread the tail through a yarn needle, and draw yarn through remaining 6 stitches and fasten off. Weave in the tail on the inside of the slipper. Weave in all remaining ends.

Following the directions on page 9, felt the slippers at the same time to the desired amount of felting.

Arrange the slippers to dry, smoothing up the sides and shaping the toes and heels as needed. Loosely stuff the slippers with plastic bags or paper toweling to help them hold their shape as they dry.

When the slippers are completely dry, pin a length of ribbon about ¼" (.6cm) down, all the way around the top edge of each slipper. Slipstitch the ribbon in place.

If you wish to make them slip-proof, attach fake suede soles to bottoms (see page 25).

Sizing Slippers

Getting felted knit slippers to fit just right can be a bit of a challenge. This is when it's particularly important to knit and felt swatches, keeping careful records of your results. (See pages 12–15 for advice on how to swatch and what to look for.)

This pattern is designed to fit a toddler. After you turn the heel, the 26 rounds that make up the gusset and foot should measure about 6½" (16.25cm). At this point you begin decreasing for the toe, but if you need a longer (or shorter) slipper, you must adjust for size *before* beginning the toe de-

creases. The 5 toe decrease rounds will measure a little more than 1" (2.5cm). Our sample shrank about 25 percent, from 8" (20cm) to 6" (15cm). Check your swatching notes. If you get about 25 percent shrinkage with your yarn and tension and felting time, you can feel confident that your finished slippers will be about 6" (15cm).

To adjust for a different amount of shrinkage or to make a longer (or shorter) slipper, add (or subtract) the number of rows you knit the foot. You should be able to estimate that each 4 rows will give you about 1" (2.5cm) of pre-felted length.

Checkerboard Slippers

This knitting pattern was popular in the 1950s, but the felted version is more shapely than its vintage ancestor. The felting process softens and hides the seams. These slippers are simple garter stitch (knit every row) on straight needles. The felt ball "buttons" are easy and fun to make, too.

YARN
Harrisville Designs Highland Style, 100% wool, worsted weight, 200 yd (183m)/3.5 oz (100g) skeins

mc   Plum (#22)
   Small: 150 yds (135m)
   Medium: 170 yds (153m)
   Large: 195 yds (178m)

cc A   Aubergine (#18)
   Small: 110 yds (99m)
   Medium: 120 yds (108m)
   Large: 130 yds (119m)

cc B   Rose (#74)
All sizes: 10 yds (9m)

NEEDLES
ONE PAIR US # 11 (8mm) straight needles, *or size you need to obtain gauge*

ADULT SIZES
Small, Medium, and Large

GAUGE, BEFORE FELTING
6½ stitches = 2" (5cm), 8 rows = 2" (5cm) in garter stitch

NUMBER OF WASH CYCLES TO ACHIEVE SAMPLE SIZE
Three

OTHER SUPPLIES
Yarn needle, red fleece and other wet felting supplies (see page 157), matching thread and needle

ABBREVIATIONS
cc   contrast color
mc   main color

APPROXIMATE MEASUREMENTS

	Before Assembling and Felting	After Felting
SMALL	13" (33cm) wide, 14" (36cm) long	8" (20cm) long, 2½ (6cm) high
MEDIUM	13" (33cm) wide, 15" (38cm) long	9" (23cm) long, 3 (7.5cm) high
LARGE	13" (33cm) wide, 16" (41cm) long	10" (25cm) long, 3½ (9cm) high

NOTE	Instructions are for one slipper. Make two identical slippers. Knit each row throughout.
SET UP	With mc, cast on 42 stitches.
ROWS 1 AND 3	Using mc, knit to end of each row.
ROWS 2 AND 4	Purl to end of each row.
ROW 5	Continuing in stockinette stitch (knit 1 row, purl 1 row, and using mc and cc A, work Checkerboard Chart (page 106), starting at the bottom right with Line 1. Take care to carry the non-working yarn loosely. For advice about knitting with two colors, see Fair Isle knitting, page 171.
NEXT ROWS	Continue to follow the chart, repeating the established pattern until the piece measures approximately 7½" (19cm) for Small, 8½" (22cm) for Medium, 9½" (24cm) for large.
	Work to the end of one of the 4-row patterns before beginning toe decreases. Knit every row in the following section (garter stitch).

DECREASING FOR THE TOE

ROWS 1–2	Using mc, knit to end of each row.
ROWS 3–4	Using cc B, knit to end of each row.
ROW 5	Using mc, *knit 5, knit 2 together; repeat from * to end of row. *You now have* 36 stitches.
ROW 6	Knit to end of row.
ROWS 7–8	Using cc A, knit to end of each row.
ROW 9	Using mc, *knit 4, knit 2 together; repeat from * to end of row. *You now have* 30 stitches.
ROW 10	Knit to end of row.
ROWS 11–12	Using cc B, knit to end of each row.

ROW 13	Using mc, *knit 3, knit 2 together; repeat from * to end of row. *You now have* 24 stitches.
ROW 14	Knit to end of row.
ROWS 15–16	Using cc A, knit to end of each row.
ROW 17	Using mc, *knit 2, knit 2 together; repeat from * to end of row. *You now have* 18 stitches.
ROW 18	Knit to end of row.
ROWS 19–20	Using cc B, knit to end of each row.
ROW 21	Using mc, *knit 1, knit 2 together; repeat from * to end of row. *You now have* 12 stitches.
ROW 22	Knit to end of row.
ROWS 23–24	Using cc A, knit to end of each row.
ROW 25	Using mc, *knit 2 together; repeat from * to end of row. *You now have* 6 stitches.
ROW 26	Knit to end of row.

Cut yarn, leaving a 20" (50cm) tail. Thread tail through a yarn needle, and draw yarn through the remaining 6 stitches. Fasten off. Cut yarn, leaving a 14" (35cm) tail.

SEWING THE SEAMS

Using the tail remaining at the toe, hold the slipper toe edges together with right sides out. Carefully match up the stripes and checkerboard patterns. Whipstitch the seam from the toe for about 7" (17.5cm) then fasten off and weave in end. (Refer to the illustration on page 106 for this step. The bunny slippers are constructed in the same way.)

With right sides still out, hold the slipper heel edges together. Starting at the upper edge, whipstitch the edges together for 4" (10cm). Bring the center bottom of the slipper up to meet the heel seam. Flatten the sides and whipstitch them together.

Following the instructions of page 9, felt the slipper to the desired size. Lay the slippers out to dry, flatten the bottoms and smooth the sides up. Smooth the toes into a uniformly rounded shape. The upper opening edges will roll slightly inward. Stuff the slippers lightly with plastic bags or paper towels, and allow them to dry thoroughly.

Using red fleece, make four felt balls (finished size about ¾"/2cm in diameter), following the instructions on page 157. Allow balls to dry, and then use matching sewing thread and needle to sew them to the slipper toe in positions shown in the photo on page 102.

Matching stripes, stitch toe edges together for about 7" (17.5cm).

Stitch heel edges together 4" (10cm) from top. Then flatten sides as shown, and stitch.

KEY

▨ MC PLUM

▨ CC A AUBERGINE

CHECKERBOARD CHART

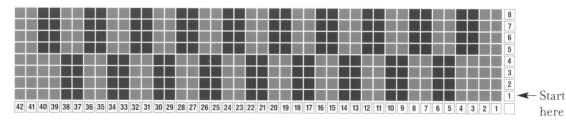

← Start here

8
7
6
5
4
3
2
1

42 41 40 39 38 37 36 35 34 33 32 31 30 29 28 27 26 25 24 23 22 21 20 19 18 17 16 15 14 13 12 11 10 9 8 7 6 5 4 3 2 1

Heather Kerner

MONTPELIER, VERMONT

A pediatric occupational therapist by trade, Vermont fiber artist Heather Kerner believes in the meditative power of repetitive crafts like knitting and felting, which she calls "replenishing" and "deeply relaxing." A crafts-woman who works in a wide range of media, from beads to wire basketry, Heather is interested in the whole process of felting, and in everything you can do with wool. Fascinated by wool in all forms, she was trained by fiber-working friends, and attended her first formal training in 2003 at Sharon Costello's Felter's Fling Conference. Heather uses every kind of wool in her work, from unwoven locks and batting to spun yarn. "Just as not all knitting projects are felted, not all felt projects are knitted," says Heather.

Heather's baskets, which she shows in juried craft shows, are made by felting and stretching wool batting around a form in hot soapy water. She explains that this is just another way of getting wool fibers to felt, and she's expanding her work to see how sculptural felt can be used to create different forms. She describes her felt vessels as somewhat like pottery. "I'm really excited to explore three-dimensional shapes."

Elaborating on her love affair with wool, she writes: "The functional potential in using a natural and renewable resource such as wool excites me. It is a material that offers an appreciation of Nature, centuries of functional and primitive uses, and the opportunity for unique design. She takes her inspiration from all kinds of fabric art, from the knitted projects of her native Maine to traditional Turkish and Mongolian patterns. Taking a cue from the traditions of other cultures, she recently started working with bold color combinations. "The magic with felt is that it's not predictable. It's a physical process, and kneading it in your hands, you see how the wool changes. You quickly get a feel for what the material can do."

Pre-felted squares, balls, dyed locks, and needle felting all make beautiful ornamentation, Heather suggests. "The possibilities are endless!" She enjoys going to sheep and wool festivals to collect new and unusual fibers. She suggests locks of wool, dyed bright colors, or with just their natural lustre, as a decoration on finished pieces. "Just play, and you'll learn what works."

Striped Slipper Socks

These striped slippers are as soft and comfy as a pair of heavy socks, and they're knitted the same way. For a variation on the pictured slippers, knit plain-color heels and toes in one of the contrasting yarns, or turn them into super-fuzzy slippers by holding a strand of brushed mohair with the worsted-weight yarn.

YARN
Harrisville Designs Highland Style, 100% wool, worsted weight, 200 yd (183m)/3.5 oz (100g) skeins

mc Poppy
    Medium: 35 yds (32m)
    Large: 45 yds (42m)

cc A Violet
    Medium: 50 yds (45m)
    Large: 70 yds (63m)

cc B Magenta
    Medium: 40 yds (36m)
    Large: 55 yds (50m)

cc C Gold
    Medium: 35 yds (32m)
    Large: 40 yds (36m)

cc D Iris
    Medium: 35 yds (32m)
    Large: 55 yds (50m)

NEEDLES
ONE SET of US #11 (8mm) double point needles, *or size you need to obtain gauge*

WOMEN'S SIZES
Medium and Large

GAUGE, BEFORE FELTING
7 stitches = 2" (5cm), 9 rows = 2" (5cm), in stockinette stitch

NUMBER OF WASH CYCLES TO ACHIEVE SAMPLE SIZE
Two

OTHER SUPPLIES
Yarn needle, stitch holder (optional)

ABBREVIATIONS
cc   contrast color

mc   main color

APPROXIMATE MEASUREMENTS

	Before Felting	After Felting
MEDIUM	13" (33cm) long, 5" (12cm) high	8½" (22cm) long, 2½" (6cm) high
LARGE	16" (41cm) long, 6½" (17cm) high	10½" (27cm) long, 3" (7.5cm) high

STARTING AT THE CUFF

		MEDIUM	LARGE
NOTE	Instructions given are for one slipper. Make two identical slippers.		
SET UP	Using mc, cast on	36 stitches	42 stitches
	Distribute the stitches evenly among three needles. Join, being careful not to twist the stitches on the needles. (For advice about knitting in the round, see page 173.)		
ROUNDS 1–2	Knit to end of each round.		
ROUND 3	Change to cc A. Knit to end of round.		
ROUND 4	Change to cc B. Knit to end of round.		

MAKING THE HEEL FLAP

		MEDIUM	LARGE
NOTE	Refer to Striped Slipper Socks Chart on page 115 for the color changes throughout project (except where noted in Turning the Heel). Cut yarns each time you begin a new stripe color, leaving a 10" (25cm) tail that you can weave in as you work, or thread through a yarn needle and weave in later. Begin working the heel flap at line 4 of chart.		
Medium size, SET UP	Needle 1: Knit 9 stitches; slide remaining stitches to Needle 2. Needle 3: Slide 9 stitches to Needle 1; slide remaining stitches to Needle 2.		
Large size, SET UP	Needle 1: Knit 10 stitches; slide remaining stitches to Needle 2. Needle 3: Slide 10 stitches to Needle 1; slide remaining stitches to Needle 2.		
Both Sizes	*You now have* the work on 2 needles, distributed as follows: Needle 1: Needle 2:	18 stitches 18 stitches	20 stitches 22 stitches

		MEDIUM	LARGE
NOTE	Work the heel flap stitches back and forth on Needle 1, turning at the end of each row. You may leave the stitches on Needle 2 or place them temporarily on a stitch holder as you work the heel flap.		
ROW 1 (WRONG SIDE)	Slip 1, purl to end of row. Turn.		
ROW 2	Slip 1, knit to end of row. Turn.		
ROW 3	Slip 1, purl to end of row. Turn.		
ROWS 4–11	Repeat Rows 2 and 3, ending at the completion of a purl row.		
NOTE	Instructions for sizes Medium and Large are given separately for the next step, Turning the Heel.		

TURNING THE HEEL, MEDIUM SIZE

		MEDIUM	LARGE
NOTE	Work this section with just mc.		
ROW 1	Slip 1, knit 9, knit 2 together, knit 1. Turn. You are leaving 5 stitches unworked on the needle.		
ROW 2	Slip 1, purl 3, purl 2 together, purl 1. Turn. You are leaving 5 stitches unworked on the needle.		
ROW 3	Slip 1, knit 4, knit 2 together, knit 1. Turn. You are leaving 3 stitches unworked on the needle.		
ROW 4	Slip 1, purl 5, purl 2 together, purl 1. Turn. You are leaving 3 stitches unworked on the needle.		
ROW 5	Slip 1, knit 6, knit 2 together, knit 1. Turn. You are leaving 1 stitch unworked on the needle.		
ROW 6	Slip 1, purl 7, purl 2 together, purl 1. Turn. You are leaving 1 stitch unworked on the needle.		

		MEDIUM	LARGE
ROW 7	Slip 1, knit 8, knit 2 together. Turn.		
ROW 8	Slip 1, purl 8, purl 2 together. Turn. All stitches are now "live" and you have	10 stitches	———

TURNING THE HEEL, LARGE SIZE

		MEDIUM	LARGE
NOTE	Work this section with just mc.		
ROW 1	Slip 1, knit 11, knit 2 together, knit 1. Turn. You are leaving 5 stitches unworked on the needle.		
ROW 2	Slip 1, purl 5, purl 2 together, purl 1. Turn. You are leaving 5 stitches unworked on the needle.		
ROW 3	Slip 1, knit 6, knit 2 together, knit 1. Turn. You are leaving 3 stitches unworked on the needle.		
ROW 4	Slip 1, purl 7, purl 2 together, purl 1. Turn. You are leaving 3 stitches unworked on the needle.		
ROW 5	Slip 1, knit 8, knit 2 together, knit 1. Turn. You are leaving 1 stitch unworked on the needle.		
ROW 6	Slip 1, purl 9, purl 2 together, purl 1. Turn. You are leaving 1 stitch unworked on the needle.		
ROW 7	Slip 1, knit 10, knit 2 together. Turn.		
ROW 8	Slip 1, purl 10, purl 2 together. Turn. All stitches are now "live" and you have	———	12 stitches

KNITTING THE INSTEP, ALL SIZES

		MEDIUM	LARGE
NOTE	The heel flap stitches that you just completed are on Needle 3. Return to your stripe pattern, picking up the sequence where you left off at the beginning of the heel flap.		
SET UP	On the heel flap (Needle 3), knit	5 stitches	6 stitches

	MEDIUM	LARGE
With an empty needle (which is now Needle 1), knit the remaining heel flap stitches:	5 stitches	6 stitches
Continuing with Needle 1, pick up and knit along the side of the heel flap	10 stitches	12 stitches
Needle 1 now has	15 stitches	18 stitches
Return to the stitches you left on Needle 2. (If you placed them on a stitch holder, replace them on Needle 2 now.) Knit the	18 stitches	22 stitches
With Needle 3, pick up and knit along the other side of the heel flap	10 stitches	12 stitches
On Needle 3, knit the remaining	5 stitches	6 stitches
You now have a total of	48 stitches	58 stitches
The stitches are distributed as follows: Needle 1:	15 stitches	18 stitches
Needle 2:	18 stitches	22 stitches
Needle 3:	15 stitches	18 stitches
ROUND 1 Knit to end of round.		
ROUND 2 Needle 1: Knit to last 2 stitches, then knit 2 together. Needle 2: Knit to end of needle. Needle 3: Knit 2 together. Knit to end of needle.		
You now have	46 stitches	56 stitches
ROUND 3 Knit to end of round.		
ROUND 4 Repeat Round 2. *You now have*	44 stitches	54 stitches
ROUND 5 Knit to end of round.		

		MEDIUM	LARGE
	Continue to knit every round (stockinette stitch) in the established stripe pattern, decreasing 2 stitches in each of the even-numbered rounds until you have	36 stitches	42 stitches

KNITTING THE FOOT

		MEDIUM	LARGE
SET UP	Redistribute the stitches evenly among the three needles. Work even in the established stripe pattern until the measurement from the back of the heel is	8" (21cm)	10" (25cm)
NOTE	To make the slippers longer, work more rounds before beginning the toe decreases. To make the slippers shorter, work fewer rounds before beginning the toe decreases.		

DECREASING FOR THE TOE

		MEDIUM	LARGE
NOTE	Large size requires 2 extra rounds at the beginning of this section.		
Large size only, EXTRA ROUND	*Knit 5, knit 2 together; repeat from * to end of round. *You now have*	——	36 stitches
Large size only, EXTRA ROUND	Knit to end of round.		
Both sizes, ROUND 1	*Knit 4, knit 2 together; repeat from * to end of round. *You now have*	30 stitches	30 stitches
ROUND 2, 4, 6, AND 8	Knit to the end of each round.		
ROUND 3	*Knit 3, knit 2 together; repeat from * to end of round. *You now have*	24 stitches	24 stitches
ROUND 5	*Knit 2, knit 2 together; repeat from * to end of round. *You now have*	18 stitches	18 stitches

		MEDIUM	LARGE
ROUND 7	*Knit 1, knit 2 together; repeat from * to end of round. *You now have*	12 stitches	12 stitches
ROUND 9	*Knit 2 together; repeat from * to end of round. *You now have*	6 stitches	6 stitches

Cut the yarn, leaving a 12" (30cm) tail. Use a yarn needle to draw the tail through the 6 remaining stitches and tighten. Weave in the tail on the inside of the slipper. Weave in any other remaining loose ends.

FINISHING

Felt both slippers at the same time, following the instructions on page 9. When the slippers are felted to the desired size, flatten their bottoms and smooth the sides up. Smooth the toes into a uniformly round shape. Stuff the slippers lightly with plastic bags or paper towels and allow them to dry thoroughly.

SLIPPER STRIPE SEQUENCE

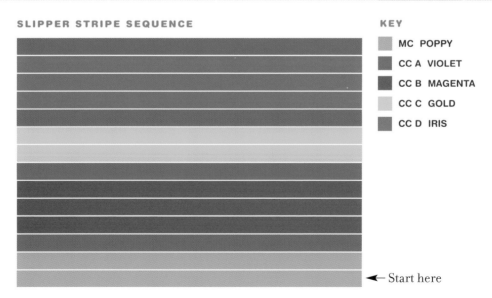

KEY

MC POPPY
CC A VIOLET
CC B MAGENTA
CC C GOLD
CC D IRIS

← Start here

Slide-On Slippers

These long-wearing slippers are sure to become favorites of the lucky owner. There's a lot of shrinkage in this yarn, but anyone who slips them on his or her feet will love the silky-softness of the thick felted slipper-socks that result.

YARN

Harrisville Designs Orchid Line, 25% mohair/5% silk/70% wool, 245 yd (224m)/3.5 oz (100g) skeins

mc   Copenhagen Blue (#233)
Child: 140 yds (126m)
Adult Small: 210 yds (189m)
Adult Medium: 240 yds (216m)

cc   Purple Quartz (#232)
Child: 35 yds (32m)
Adult Small: 40 yds (36m)
Adult Medium: 50 yds (45m)

NEEDLES

ONE SET US #11 (8mm) double point needles, *or size you need to obtain gauge*

SIZES

Child, Adult Small, and Adult Medium

GAUGE, BEFORE FELTING

6 stitches = 2" (5cm), 8 rows = 2" (5cm) in stockinette stitch

NUMBER OF WASH CYCLES TO ACHIEVE SAMPLE SIZE

Two

OTHER SUPPLIES

Yarn needle

ABBREVIATIONS

cc   contrast color

mc   main color

APPROXIMATE MEASUREMENTS

	Before Felting	After Felting
CHILD	14" (36cm) long, 6½" (17cm) high	6½" (17cm) long, 2" (5cm) high
ADULT SMALL	16" (41cm) long, 8½" (22cm) high	7½" (19cm) long, 2½" (6cm) high
ADULT MEDIUM	18" (16cm) long, 10" (25cm) high	10" (25cm) long, 3" (7.5cm) high

KNITTING THE SIDES

		CHILD	ADULT SMALL	ADULT MEDIUM
NOTE	Instructions are for one slipper. Knit two identical slippers.			
	Using a single strand of cc yarn, cast on	36 stitches	42 stitches	48 stitches
	Divide the stitches evenly among three needles, and join to knit in the round. For knitting in the round, see page 173.			
ROUNDS 1–2	Knit to end of each round.			

DIVIDING FOR THE HEEL

Child size only — Knit 9 stitches from Needle 1. Slide the remaining 3 stitches onto Needle 2. Slide 9 stitches from Needle 3 onto Needle 1. Slide the remaining 3 stitches from Needle 3 onto Needle 2. Needles 1 and 2 each have 18 stitches. Set Needle 2 aside.

Adult Small size only — Knit 10 stitches from Needle 1. Slide the remaining 4 stitches onto Needle 2. Slide 10 stitches from Needle 3 onto Needle 1. Slide the remaining 4 stitches from Needle 3 onto Needle 2. Needle 1 (heel flap needle) now has 20 stitches; Needle 2 has 22 stitches.

Adult Medium size only — Knit 11 stitches from Needle 1. Slide the remaining 5 stitches onto Needle 2. Slide 11 stitches from Needle 3 onto Needle 1. Slide the remaining 5 stitches from Needle 3 onto Needle 2. Needle 1 (heel flap needle) now has 22 stitches; Needle 2 has 26 stitches.

WORKING THE HEEL FLAP

All sizes — In this section, work back and forth in stockinette stitch (knit 1 row, turn, purl 1 row, turn) on Needle 1 only.

ROW 1 — Change to mc. Slip 1 stitch, purl to end of row. Turn.

ROW 2 — Slip 1 stitch, knit to end of row. Turn.

ROWS 3–11	Repeat Rows 1 and 2. End when you have completed a purl row.
Adult Medium size only,	
ROWS 12–13	Repeat Rows 1 and 2. End when you have completed a purl row.
NOTE	In the next section, directions for the sizes are given separately.

TURNING THE HEEL, CHILD SIZE ONLY

ROW 1	Change to cc. Slip 1 stitch, knit 9, knit 2 together, knit 1, turn. Leave 5 stitches unworked.
ROW 2	Slip 1 stitch, purl 3, purl 2 together, purl 1, turn. Leave 5 stitches unworked.
ROW 3	Slip 1 stitch, knit 4, knit 2 together, knit 1, turn. Leave 3 stitches unworked.
ROW 4	Slip 1 stitch, purl 5, purl 2 together, purl 1, turn. Leave 3 stitches unworked.
ROW 5	Slip 1 stitch, knit 6, knit 2 together, knit 1, turn. Leave 1 stitch unworked.
ROW 6	Slip 1 stitch, purl 7, purl 2 together, purl 1, turn. Leave 1 stitch unworked.
ROW 7	Slip 1 stitch, knit 8, knit 2 together, turn.
ROW 8	Purl 9, knit 2 together. *You now have* 10 "live" stitches.

TURNING THE HEEL, ADULT SMALL SIZE ONLY

ROW 1	Change to cc. Slip 1 stitch, knit 11, knit 2 together, knit 1, turn. Leave 5 stitches unworked.
ROW 2	Slip 1 stitch, purl 5, purl 2 together, purl 1, turn. Leave 5 stitches unworked.
ROW 3	Slip 1 stitch, knit 6, knit 2 together, knit 1, turn. Leave 3 stitches unworked.
ROW 4	Slip 1 stitch, purl 7, purl 2 together, purl 1 turn. Leave 3 stitches unworked.
ROW 5	Slip 1 stitch, knit 8, knit 2 together, knit 1, turn. Leave 1 stitch unworked.
ROW 6	Slip 1 stitch, purl 9, purl 2 together, purl 1, turn. Leave 1 stitch unworked.
ROW 7	Slip 1 stitch, knit 10, knit 2 together, turn.
ROW 8	Purl 11, purl 2 together. *You now have* 12 "live" stitches.

ROW 1	Change to cc. Slip 1 stitch, knit 12, knit 2 together, knit 1, turn. Leave 6 stitches unworked.
ROW 2	Slip 1 stitch, purl 5, purl 2 together, purl 1, turn. Leave 6 stitches unworked.
ROW 3	Slip 1 stitch, knit 6, knit 2 together, knit 1, turn. Leave 4 stitches unworked.
ROW 4	Slip 1 stitch, purl 7, purl 2 together, purl 1, turn. Leave 4 stitches unworked.
ROW 5	Slip 1 stitch, knit 8, knit 2 together, knit 1, turn. Leave 2 stitches unworked.
ROW 6	Slip 1 stitch, purl 9, purl 2 together, purl 1, turn. Leave 2 stitches unworked.
ROW 7	Slip 1 stitch, knit 10, knit 2 together, knit 1, turn.
ROW 8	Purl 12, purl 2 together, purl 1. *You now have 14 "live" stitches.*

KNITTING THE GUSSET

		CHILD	ADULT SMALL	ADULT MEDIUM
NOTE	Starting here, you will again knit in the round.			
ROW 1: SET UP ROUND	Knit	5 stitches	6 stitches	7 stitches
NOTE	The just-knit stitches will be used later on Needle 3.			
	Change to mc. Using an empty needle, knit the remaining	5 stitches	6 stitches	7 stitches
	The needle containing the just-knit stitches is now Needle 1.			

	CHILD	ADULT SMALL	ADULT MEDIUM
With Needle 1, pick up along the side of the heel flap	10 stitches	12 stitches	13 stitches
From Needle 2 (the stitches held aside while you were knitting the heel flap), knit the	18 stitches	22 stitches	26 stitches
With Needle 3, pick up along the other side of the heel flap	10 stitches	12 stitches	13 stitches
Knit the remaining stitches onto Needle 3:	5 stitches	6 stitches	7 stitches
The stitches are now divided as follows:			
Needle 1:	15 stitches	18 stitches	20 stitches
Needle 2:	18 stitches	22 stitches	26 stitches
Needle 3:	15 stitches	18 stitches	20 stitches

ROUND 2 Knit to end of round.

ROUND 3 Needle 1: Knit to the last 2 stitches, knit 2 stitches together.
Needle 2: Knit to end of needle.
Needle 3: Knit 2 together, knit to end of needle.

	CHILD	ADULT SMALL	ADULT MEDIUM
NEXT ROUNDS Repeat Rounds 2 and 3	5 more times	7 more times	8 more times
You now have			
Needle 1:	9 stitches	10 stitches	11 stitches
Needle 2:	18 stitches	22 stitches	26 stitches
Needle 3:	9 stitches	10 stitches	11 stitches

KNITTING THE FOOT

	CHILD	ADULT SMALL	ADULT MEDIUM
SET UP Evenly distribute the stitches among the needles.	36 stitches	42 stitches	48 stitches
NEXT ROUNDS Continuing to use mc, knit to the end of each round until slipper measured from the back of the heel is	8" (21cm)	10" (26cm)	12" (31cm)

	CHILD	ADULT SMALL	ADULT MEDIUM
NOTE — Adult Medium requires 4 extra rounds and Adult Small requires 2 extra rounds at the beginning of this section.			
Adult Medium size only, **EXTRA ROUND** — Change to cc. *Knit 6, knit 2 together; repeat from * to end of round. *You now have*			42 stitches
Adult Medium size only, **EXTRA ROUND** — Knit to end of round.			
Adult sizes only, **EXTRA ROUND** — Using cc, *knit 5, knit 2 together; repeat from * to end of round. *You now have*	——	36 stitches	36 stitches
Adult sizes only, **EXTRA ROUND** — Knit to end of round.			
All sizes, **ROUND 1** — Change to cc. *Knit 4, knit 2 together; repeat from * to end of round. *You now have*	30 stitches	30 stitches	30 stitches
ROUNDS 2, 4, 6, AND 8 — Knit to end of each round.			
ROUND 3 — *Knit 3, knit 2 together; repeat from * to end of round. *You now have*	24 stitches	24 stitches	24 stitches
ROUND 5 — *Knit 2, knit 2 together; repeat from * to end of round. *You now have*	18 stitches	18 stitches	18 stitches
ROUND 7 — *Knit 1, knit 2 together; repeat from * to end of round. *You now have*	12 stitches	12 stitches	12 stitches
ROUND 9 — *Knit 2 together; repeat from * to end of round. *You now have*	6 stitches	6 stitches	6 stitches

Cut yarn, leaving a 12" (30cm) tail. Thread the tail through a yarn needle, and draw yarn through the remaining 6 stitches. Fasten off. Weave in all loose ends on the wrong side of the slipper.

Felt both slippers at the same time according to the instructions on page 9. When slippers are felted as desired, flatten the slipper bottoms and smooth the sides up. Smooth the toes into a uniformly rounded shape. Stuff the slippers with plastic bags or paper towels, then allow them to dry completely.

Kristiane Kristensen

EAST BURKE, VERMONT

With a background in clothing and costume design and construction, Kristiane Kristensen is fascinated by the range of possibilities for using felt in garments, as well as the characteristics of felt that make it possible to create the actual fabric for a given piece. Hats are her primary focus, but she is also eagerly experimenting with designing single-piece (no-sew) vests and jackets.

Kristiane uses felt made directly from the fleece, rather than first being knitted or woven. She washes, dyes, and cards (a process that aligns and fluffs up the fleece) wool sheep fleece, then felts it, working the piece into its final shape.

Kristiane enjoys the fact that the ancient craft of felting is still around today. She points out that each of the stages involved in the preparation and creation of a felted object can be done in numerous different ways, allowing the artist to use any one of many traditional techniques or combination of techniques.

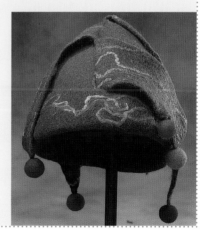

5 Felt Around the House

Striped Teddy Bear

This soft, cuddly bear will appeal just as much to teens as to toddlers. We've embroidered the buttons and facial features, so there are no small pieces to worry about with young children, but you may wish to use buttons or other decorative notions if safety is not a concern.

YARN
Harrisville Designs Highland Style, 100% wool, worsted weight, 200 yd (183m)/3.5 oz (100g) skeins

mc	90 yds (82m) Poppy
cc A	60 yds (54m) Iris
cc B	20 yds (18m) Magenta

Brown Sheep Lamb's Pride, worsted weight, 192 yd (176m)/ 4 oz (113g) skeins

cc C	25 yds (23m) Limeade

NEEDLES
ONE SET US #13 (9mm) double point needles, *or size you need to obtain gauge*

GAUGE, BEFORE FELTING
6 stitches = 2" (5cm), 7 rows = 2" (5cm), using 2 strands of worsted yarn in stockinette stitch

NUMBER OF WASH CYCLES TO ACHIEVE SAMPLE SIZE
Two

OTHER SUPPLIES:
One stitch holder, two stitch markers, yarn needle, polyester fiberfill, matching sewing thread and needle, 20" (50cm) bright pink wool crewel yarn, ¾" (2cm) wide magenta grosgrain ribbon

ABBREVIATIONS

cc	contrast color
mc	main color

APPROXIMATE MEASUREMENTS

Before Felting
12" (31 cm) from neck to toe, 6½" (17cm) wide

After Felting
12" (31cm) from top of head to toe, 4¾" (12cm) wide

KNITTING THE BODY FROM THE NECK DOWN

NOTE	For an illustration of how to "make 1" in the following section, see page 172.
SET UP	Using 2 strands of cc A and double point needles, cast on 18 stitches. Divide the stitches evenly among three needles. Join, being careful not to twist the stitches. (See page 173 for advice about knitting in the round.) Continue to use 2 strands of yarn throughout project.
ROUNDS 1–2	Knit to end of each round.
ROUND 3	*Knit 3, make 1; repeat from * to end of round. *You now have* 24 stitches.
ROUND 4	Change to 2 strands of cc C. Knit to end of round.
ROUND 5	Change to 2 strands of cc A. Knit to end of round.
ROUND 6	*Knit 4, make 1; repeat from * to end of round. *You now have* 30 stitches.
ROUND 7	Change to 2 strands of cc C. Knit to end of round.
ROUNDS 8–9	Change to 2 strands of cc A. Knit to end of each round.
ROUNDS 10–15	Repeat Rounds 7–9 two more times.
ROUNDS 16–19	Change to 2 strands of mc. Knit to end of each round.

KNITTING THE FIRST LEG

SET UP	Still using 2 strands of mc, knit 15 and place those stitches on a stitch holder. Divide the remaining stitches among three needles as follows:
	Needle 1: 6 stitches Needle 2: 6 stitches Needle 3: 3 stitches
	On Needle 3, cast on 3 more stitches. Join stitches in a round, taking care not to twist stitches. *You now have* 18 stitches.
ROUNDS 1–12	Knit to end of each round.

ROUND 13	Change to 2 strands of cc A. Knit to end of round.
ROUND 14	Change to 2 strands of cc C. Knit to end of round.
ROUND 15	Change to 2 strands of cc A. Knit to end of round.
ROUND 16	Change to 2 strands of cc B. *Knit 1, knit 2 together; repeat from * to end of round. *You now have* 12 stitches.
ROUND 17	Knit to end of round.
ROUND 18	*Knit 2 together; repeat from * to end of round. *You now have* 6 stitches.

Cut yarn, leaving a 10" (25cm) tail. Thread tail through a yarn needle and draw yarn through the remaining 6 stitches. Fasten off and weave tail in on inside of leg.

KNITTING THE SECOND LEG

With the stitches you set aside on the holder, repeat the Set Up and Rounds 1–18 under Knitting the First Leg.

KNITTING THE ARMS

NOTE	Make two identical arms.
SET UP	Using 2 strands of cc A, cast on 15 stitches. Divide the stitches evenly among three needles. Join in the round, being careful not to twist any stitches.
ROUNDS 1–2	With 2 strands of cc A, knit to end of each round.
ROUND 3	Change to 2 strands of cc C. Knit to end of round.
ROUNDS 4–12	Repeat Rounds 1-3 three more times.
ROUND 13	Change to 2 strands of cc A. *Knit 1, knit 2 together; repeat from * to end of round. *You now have* 10 stitches.
ROUND 14	Change to 2 strands of cc B. Knit to end of round.
ROUND 15	*Knit 2 together; repeat from * to end of round. *You now have* 5 stitches.

Cut yarn, leaving a 10" (25 cm) tail. Thread the tail through a yarn needle, and draw yarn through remaining 6 stitches. Fasten off and weave in tail on the inside of the arm.

KNITTING THE HEAD

SET UP	Using 2 strands of mc, cast on 18 stitches. Divide the stitches evenly among three needles. Join, being careful not to twist stitches.
ROUNDS 1–2	Knit to end of each round.
ROUND 3	*Knit 3, make 1; repeat from * to end of round. *You now have* 24 stitches.
ROUNDS 4, 6, AND 8	Knit to end of each round.
ROUND 5	Knit 1, place a stitch marker on the needle, make 1, knit 1, make 1, place another stitch marker on the needle, knit to end of round. *You now have* 26 stitches.
ROUND 7	Knit 1, slide stitch marker, make 1, knit to next stitch marker, make 1, slide stitch marker, knit to end of round. *You now have* 28 stitches.
ROUND 9–10	Repeat Rounds 7-8. *You now have* 30 stitches.
ROUND 11	Knit to end of round.
ROUND 12	Knit 1, slide stitch marker, knit 2 together, knit to 2 stitches before next stitch marker, knit 2 together, slide stitch marker, knit to end of round. *You now have* 28 stitches.
ROUNDS 13, 15, 17, 19, AND 21	Knit to end of each round.
ROUND 14	Repeat Round 12. *You now have* 26 stitches.
ROUND 16	Knit 1, remove stitch marker, knit 3 stitches together, remove next stitch marker, knit to end of round. *You now have* 24 stitches.
ROUND 18	*Knit 2, knit 2 together; repeat from * to end of round. *You now have* 18 stitches.

ROUND 20	*Knit 1, knit 2 together; repeat from * to end of round. *You now have* 12 stitches.
ROUND 22	*Knit 2 together; repeat from * to end of round. *You now have* 6 stitches.
	Cut yarn, leaving a 10" (25cm) tail. Thread yarn through yarn needle, and draw yarn through the remaining stitches. Fasten off. Weave in tail on inside of head.

KNITTING THE EARS

NOTE	The ears are knit back and forth in stockinette stitch (knit one row, turn, purl one row). Since there are so few stitches, you may use two of your double point needles for this section.
SET UP	With cc A, cast on 12 stitches.
ROW 1	Knit to end of row. Turn.
ROW 2	Purl to end of row. Turn.
ROW 3	Change to cc B. Knit to end of row. Turn.
ROWS 4, 6, AND 8	Purl to end of each row. Turn.
ROW 5	Knit to end of row. Turn.
ROW 7	*Knit 2, knit 2 together; repeat from * to end of row. Turn. *You now have* 9 stitches.
ROW 9	*Knit 1, knit 2 together; repeat from * to end of row. *You now have* 6 stitches.
	Bind off. Weave in all loose ends.

FINISHING

Felt all body pieces together, following instructions on page 9. When the pieces have felted as desired, smooth them out on a flat surface. Shape head and nose gusset. Flatten ears. Allow pieces to dry completely before assembling.

Using cc B, embroider a French knot on each cc C stripe.

Using polyester fiberfill, loosely stuff the bear's body and legs, arms, and head. *Note:* For a more cuddly toy, do not stuff the bear too tightly. Use a knitting needle to stuff the fiberfill into the crevices, if necessary.

Using matching sewing thread, sew the arms into place, 1" (2.5cm) from the neck edge. Sew the head in place on the neck.

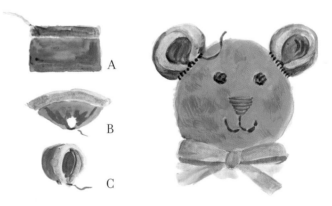

Following the illustration, use cc A to embroider French-knot eyes on the bear's head. Using bright pink crewel yarn, embroider a satin-stitch nose. Using cc B, embroider a smiling mouth, using a backstitch.

Fold the lower ear corners in (see above A and B), then bring the top corners down to meet the lower corners (C). With matching thread, tack corners in place at top of head, then stitch them all around. Make a grosgrain ribbon bow at the neck.

Crispina ffrench

Born in Ireland and raised in Western Massachusetts, where she now resides, Crispina ffrench has a fine arts degree from the Massachusetts College of Art in Boston. During her sophomore year, Crispina created a collection of handwoven clothing and Ragamuffins, whimsical dolls made from recycled wool sweaters, which she sold through a craft cooperative in Cambridge, Massachusetts. This business, plus two other part-time jobs allowed her to graduate from college debt-free. Her success at The American Craft Council Exhibit in West Springfield, Massachusetts, launched her business with flying colors.

Her current company, Fuchsia, Inc. dba Crispina, recycles wool sweaters and worn denim jeans into heirloom-quality blankets, throws, pillows, rugs, and window treatments. Crispina is founder and Creative Director of Fuchsia, whose mission is to promote "sustainability by turning throwaways into treasure." In their Housatonic riverbank studio, Crispina and her colleagues wash, sort, cut, combine, sew, and press using a special process designed to enhance the natural qualities of the fabrics, making the finished products remarkably plush, soft, warm, comforting, and durable. Her business recently received RIRC grants from the Massachusetts Department of Environmental Protection.

Crispina likes to "celebrate the quirks of the original garments," by creatively including features like pockets, buttons, and labels in the recycled item. Her products have been featured in such publications as *The New York Times, Country Home, Traditional Home, Country Living,* and *Organic Style.* Crispina, Inc. has reclaimed more than 200,000 pounds of discarded clothing — truly spinning straw into gold!

Pillow Gridlock

This pillow is fun to knit using a technique known as intarsia, which uses a separate ball of yarn for each color block. When you pick up a new color to begin the next block, be sure to wrap the new yarn around the old one, to avoid getting holes at the color changes. See page 172 for more information.

YARN
Brown Sheep Lamb's Pride, 85% wool/15% mohair, worsted weight, 190 yd (173m)/4 oz (113g) skeins

mc   25 yds (23m)
Grey Heather (#03)

cc A   100 yds (90m)
Charcoal Heather (#04)

cc B   100 yds (90m)
Deep Charcoal (#06)

NEEDLES
ONE SET US #11 (8mm) straight needles, 14" (35cm) long, *or size you need to obtain gauge*

SIZE
12" x 16" (30cm x 40cm)

GAUGE, BEFORE FELTING
6.5 stitches = 2" (10cm), 8 rows = 2" in stockinette stitch

WASH CYCLES NEEDED TO ACHIEVE FINISHED SIZE
Three

OTHER SUPPLIES
Yarn needle, ½ yd (.5m) fabric for pillow backing, matching sewing thread, pins and needle, 12" x 16" (30cm x 40cm) pillow form or polyester fiberfill, red fleece for making four 1" (2.5cm) balls

ABBREVIATIONS
cc   contrast color

mc   main color

APPROXIMATE MEASUREMENTS

Before Felting

19½" (50cm) wide, 20½" (52cm) tall

After Felting

14½" (37cm) wide, 13" (33cm) tall

NOTE

You will be casting on 20 stitches of each color yarn in preparation for intarsia knitting (see page 172). Wind off two approximately equal-size balls each of cc A and cc B before beginning to knit. Leave a 10" (25cm) tail each time you change colors when casting on. Weave the tails in later. If the tails get in your way when you're knitting the first few rows, or if you have trouble maintaining tension, you can tie them together temporarily until your work is established. Untie the knots and weave in the ends later. Refer to photo on page 134 for guidance in color changes.

With cc A, cast on 20 stitches.

Drop cc A, and on the same needle use cc B to cast on 20 stitches.

Drop cc B, and on the same needle use second ball of cc A to cast on 20 stitches. You now have 60 stitches.

ROW 1

Knit 20 stitches with cc A. Pick up cc B and twist it around cc A, then knit 20 stitches with cc B, leaving cc A behind. Pick up cc A and twist it around cc B, then knit 20 stitches with cc A, leaving cc B behind.

ROW 2

Following the pattern established in Row 1, purl 20 with cc A, purl 20 with cc B, purl 20 with cc A. Be sure to twist strands together on the wrong (purl) side of the knitting.

ROWS 3–28

Repeat Rows 1 and 2. Cut all yarns, leaving 5" (12.5 cm) tails to weave in later.

ROW 29

Change to cc B and knit 20. Change to mc and knit 20. Change to cc B and knit 20. Leave 5" (12.5cm) tails to weave in later.

ROWS 30–56

Continue working in the established pattern. Cut all yarns, leaving 5" (12.5cm) tails.

Changing Colors

When you wrap the old and new yarns around each other at each color break, be sure to make the wrap on the wrong side, whether you are knitting or purling.

KNITTING THE THIRD ROW OF BLOCKS

ROWS 57–84   Repeat rows 1–28.

Cast off. Cut yarn and weave in all loose ends on the wrong side of the work.

FELTING THE PILLOW TOP

Felt the piece, following the instructions on page 9. Check the progress regularly, and take that opportunity to stretch the pillow top to help maintain even edges and uniform color blocks.

SHAPING THE PILLOW TOP

Smooth the pillow top on a flat surface. Stretch it as necessary, making sure all edges are even, corners form 90-degree angles, and color blocks are straight. Use T-pins to hold its shape while it is drying.

ASSEMBLING THE PILLOW TOP

Lay the pillow top on the pillow-backing fabric with right sides together. Pin the pillow top to the backing fabric and use large stitches to baste them together.

With a sewing machine or by hand, sew the pillow top to the backing around the outside edge, leaving a ¼" (.6cm) seam allowance. Leave an 8" (20cm) opening in the center of one of the short sides.

Trim the excess fabric from the sewn pillow top and turn the top right side out, using a knitting needle to push the corners out if necessary.

Put the pillow form into the pillow covering. Turn the raw opening edges in and slipstitch the pillow top closed.

Following the instructions on page 157, make four red felt balls, each about ¾" in diameter. When the balls are dry, use sewing thread to tack them to the pillow, refering to the photo on page 134 for placement. If you prefer, you can use purchased buttons instead of the felt balls.

Novelty Yarn Pillows

If you're looking for interesting textures and effects, search no further than your nearest yarn store. Here we feature a fur-look, tufted chenille-like polka dot, hand-dyed yarns, backed with coordinating silk fabrics.

YARN FOR PILLOW 1 (BOTTOM)
cc A Manos del Uruguay, 100% wool, 138 yd (126m)/3.5 oz (100g) skeins
    250 yds (229m)   Raspberry

YARN FOR PILLOW 2 (CENTER)
cc B Nordic Fiber Arts Rauma Vamsegarn, 100% wool, 3-ply, 91 yd (83m)/1.75 oz (50g) skeins
    180 yds (165m)   #V24 (red)

cc C Crystal Palace Fizz, 100% polyester, 120 yd (110m)/1.75 oz (50g) balls
    90 yds (82m)   #08 (red)

YARN FOR PILLOW 3 (TOP)
cc D Harrisville Designs Highland Style, 100% wool, 200 yd (183m)/3.5 oz (100g) skeins
    190 yds (171m)   Iris

cc E Berroco Bubble FX, 62% acrylic/38% nylon, 168 yd (155m)/.875 oz (25g) balls
    190 yds (17m)   #8425

NEEDLES
ONE PAIR US #11 (8mm) straight needles, 12" (30cm) long, *or size you need to obtain gauge*

GAUGE, BEFORE FELTING
(All gauges in stockinette stitch with the pattern yarn or yarns)
Pillow 1: 6 stitches = 2" (5cm), 8 rows = 2" (5cm) using cc A
Pillow 2: 6 stitches = 2" (5cm), 8 rows = 2" (5cm) using cc B, held together with cc C on alternate rows

Pillow 3: 6 stitches = 2" (5cm), 8 rows = 2" (5cm), using cc D and cc E held together throughout

NUMBER OF WASH CYCLES TO ACHIEVE SAMPLE SIZE
Pillow 1: One
Pillow 2: Two
Pillow 3: Two

OTHER SUPPLIES
Yarn needle, polyester pillow forms (Pillow 1, 14" x 14"/35 x 35cm; Pillow 2, 12" x 16"/30 x 40cm; Pillow 3, 12" x 12"/30 x 30cm), ½ yd (.5m) per pillow coordinating silk or other fabric for backing, matching sewing thread and needle, tassels (optional)

ABBREVIATIONS
cc   contrast color

APPROXIMATE MEASUREMENTS

	Before Felting	After Felting
PILLOW 1	22" (56cm) wide, 23" (57cm) tall	14" (36cm) wide, 14" (36cm) tall
PILLOW 2	22" (56cm) wide, 18" (45cm) tall	16" (41cm) wide, 12" (31cm) tall
PILLOW 3	19" (47cm) wide, 21" (54cm) tall	12" (31cm) wide, 12" (31cm) tall

KNITTING PILLOW 1

SET UP	Using cc A, cast on 66 stitches.
ROW 1	Knit to end of row.
ROW 2	Purl to end of row.
ROWS 3–90	Repeat Rows 1 and 2.
	Bind off. Cut yarn, leaving a 10" (25cm) tail. Thread tail through a yarn needle and weave in on wrong side of work.

KNITTING PILLOW 2

SET UP	Using cc B, cast on 66 stitches.
NOTE	The cc C yarn is worked only on odd-numbered rows. Because the piece is seamed when the knitting is completed, you can simply cut cc C at the end of the rows where it is worked and leave the tail. (Even without seaming, the novelty yarn is held securely in place by the wool yarn when it is felted.)
ROW 1	Using cc B and cc C held together, knit to end of row. Cut cc C, leaving a 2" (5cm) tail.
ROW 2	Using cc B only, purl to end of row.
ROWS 3–70	Repeat Rows 1 and 2, working cc C only on even-numbered rows, cutting it at the end of the each row.
	Bind off. Cut yarn, leaving a 10" (25 cm) tail. Thread tail through a yarn needle and weave in tail on wrong side of work.

KNITTING PILLOW 3

SET UP	Using cc D and cc E, cast on 56 stitches.
ROW 1	Using cc D and cc E held together, knit to end of row.
ROW 2	Continuing to use both yarns, purl to end of row.
ROWS 3–84	Repeat Rows 1 and 2.

Bind off. Cut yarn, leaving a 10" (25 cm) tail. Thread tail through a yarn needle and weave in on wrong side of work.

FINISHING

Following the instructions on page 9, felt the knitted pillow fabric.

When the desired degree of felting has been achieved, lay the felted pieces out to dry on a flat surface. Smooth and stretch the pieces, making sure all corners are square and edges are even. Pin the piece along the edges to hold their shape until dry. (See page 11 for further advice.)

Measure the pieces. Allowing for a 1" (2.5cm) seam all around, they should be 2" (5cm) wider and longer than the measurement of the pillow form. Trim as needed.

Lay the felted piece on the backing fabric, and cut the backing to match.

Sew around all four sides, using a 1" (2.5cm) seam, and leaving a 6" (15cm) opening on one side.

Push the pillow form through the opening. Fold the raw edges of the opening to the inside, and slipstitch the edges together.

If you wish, decorate the corners with tassels.

Wine Sack

The next time you go on a picnic — or the invitation says BYO — carry your wine along in this elegant bag. The soft, thick felt will keep the bottle well protected, and even contribute some insulation. The grape "vine" and grape leaf "veins" are applied using a technique known as needle felting. The "grapes" are made by felting fleece (see page 157 for directions).

YARNS
Harrisville Designs Highland Style, 100% wool, worsted weight, 200 yd (183m)/3.5 oz (100g) skeins

mc	280 yds (252m)	Bluegrass
cc A	25 yds (23m)	Olive
cc B	50 yds (46m)	Hemlock

NEEDLES
ONE US #13 (9mm) circular needle, 16–18" (40–45cm) long, *or size you need to obtain gauge*

ONE SET double point needles, two sizes smaller

GAUGE, BEFORE FELTING
6 stitches = 2" (5cm), 8 rows = 2" (5cm) on larger needles, using a double strand of yarn

NUMBER OF WASH CYCLES TO ACHIEVE SAMPLE SIZE
Two

OTHER SUPPLIES
Yarn needle, point protectors, permanent marker, approximately 1 yd (.9m) black or dark brown sport weight yarn, purple fleece and wet felt supplies (see page 157), crochet hook, felting needle, 3" (8cm) sponge, sewing needle and matching sewing thread

ABBREVIATIONS

cc	contrast color
mc	main color

APPROXIMATE MEASUREMENTS

Before Felting
6½" (17cm) wide, 20" (51cm) long

After Felting
5½" (14cm) wide, 16" (41cm) tall

SET UP	Using two strands of mc and the double point needles, cast on 3 stitches. Turn.
ROUND 1	Increase 1 stitch in each stitch by knitting into the front and back of it. *You now have* 6 stitches. Distribute these stitches evenly among three double point needles and join them into a round. (For information about knitting in the round, see page 173.)
ROUND 2	Knit to end of round.
ROUND 3	Increase 1 stitch in each of the 6 stitches by knitting into the front and back of each stitch. *You now have* 12 stitches.
ROUND 4	Knit to end of round.
ROUND 5	*Knit 1, increase 1 by knitting into the front and back of the next stitch; repeat from * to end of round. *You now have* 18 stitches.
ROUND 6	Knit to end of round.
ROUND 7	*Knit 2, increase 1 by knitting into the front and back of the next stitch; repeat from * to end of round. *You now have* 24 stitches.
ROUND 8	Knit to end of round.
ROUND 9	*Knit 3, increase 1 by knitting into the front and back of the next stitch; repeat from * to end of round. *You now have* 30 stitches.
ROUND 10	Knit to end of round.
ROUND 11	*Knit 4, increase 1 by knitting into the front and back of the next stitch; repeat from * to end of round. *You now have* 36 stitches.
ROUND 12	Knit to end of round.
ROUND 13	*Knit 5, increase 1 by knitting into the front and back of the next stitch; repeat from * to end of round. *You now have* 42 stitches.
ROUND 14	Knit to end of round.
ROUND 15	Purl to end of round.

KNITTING THE SIDES

Change to the circular needle. Place a marker to indicate beginning of round.

NEXT ROUNDS Knit to end of each round until piece measures 18" (46cm) from purl row.

KNITTING THE TOP

**ROUND 1
(EYELET ROUND)** *Knit 5, knit 2 together, yarn over; repeat from * to end of round. *You still have* 42 stitches, counting each yarn over as a stitch.(For explanation of how to "yarn over," see page 174.

ROUND 2 Knit to end of round, knitting the yarn overs of the preceding round as normal stitches.

NEXT ROUNDS Knit to end of each round until entire piece measures 20" (51cm) from the purl row.

Cast off, leaving a 10" (25cm) tail. Thread the tail through a yarn needle, and weave it into the wrong side of the bag, neatly closing the gap between the first and last cast-off stitches.

KNITTING THE I-CORD TIE

SET UP Using a single strand of cc A and two double point needles, cast on 3 stitches.

Knit a 30" (76cm) long I-cord, following the instructions for I-cord on page 171.

Cut the yarn, leaving a 10" (25cm) tail. Thread the tail through a yarn needle, and weave it up inside the I-cord. Weave in the cast-on tail the same way.

MAKING THE LEAF APPLIQUÉ

NOTE The appliqué fabric is worked in stockinette stitch (knit 1 row, turn, purl 1 row, turn). To avoid purchasing straight needles for this small piece, place point protectors (or wrap a small rubber band) on one end of two double point needles and use them as straight needles.

SET UP Using two of the double point needles and a single strand of cc B, cast on 30 stitches.

ROW 1	Knit to end of row.
ROW 2	Purl to end of row.
NEXT ROWS	Repeat Rows 1 and 2 until piece measures 10" (25cm) from cast-on edge.

Cast off, leaving a 10" (25cm) tail. Thread the tail through a yarn needle, and weave it into the wrong side. Weave in any other tails.

FINISHING THE SACK

Following the instructions on page 9, felt the sack, I-cord tie, and leaf applique swatch together, as desired.

Slip the felted sack over a wine bottle a size larger than you anticipate normally carrying in the sack. Using a mold not only helps maintain the correct size, but also avoids setting permanent creases in the sides. Smooth the sack over the bottle, aligning the purl row around the base and making sure the top edge is even and that the stitches are parallel to the vertical lines of the bottle.

Lay out I-cord tie, smoothing and pulling it to stretch it as needed.

Lay out swatch for leaf applique, smoothing it, squaring the corners, and stretching the sides as needed to create an even square.

DECORATING THE SACK

Trace leaf pattern at right. Place the pattern on the wrong side of the felted appliqué swatch and use a permanent marker to trace around it. Cut out the leaf.

Referring to the photo on page 142 for placement, pin the leaf to the sack. Using a sewing needle and matching thread, sew the leaf to the sack with small running stitches about ¼" (6mm) from the edge all the way around. The stitches will become

LEAF TEMPLATE

buried in the felt, but the small indentation that remains adds to the sculptural effect of the leaf.

Referring to the photo on page 142 for placement, pin strands of black or dark brown sport weight yarn on the leaf to create vein-like outlines. Place a 3" (8cm) sponge under the work. Then, holding a felting needle straight up and down, poke the needle through the yarn and fabric, working along the length of the yarn, until the yarn is firmly felted to the underlying fabric (see illustration at right).

Needle felting

Referring to the photo on page 142, pin a strand of cc A around the sack to create the grapevine. Needle felt the yarn in place, as described above.

Following the instructions for making felt balls on page 157, make 11 oval (grape-shaped) balls, each about 1" (2.5cm) long. Allow these to dry before attaching them to the sack.

To create a structure to attach the "grapes" to, use cc A to single crochet a chain about 3½" (9cm) long. Add two or three short (about 1"/2.5cm) "arms" to the chain, 2" (5cm) and 2½" (6cm) from the top of the chain.

Use a yarn needle to weave all tails back into the chain. Use a sewing needle and matching thread to tack the short ends of the "grapes" along the crocheted stems to create a bunch of grapes.

Referring to the photo for placement, use a sewing needle and matching thread to tack the crocheted stem to the sack. The "grapes" should hang freely.

Weave the I-cord tie through the eyelets at the top of the bag. You may need to open the eyelets with a knitting needle to free the holes. The ties should begin and end over the grape ornaments.

Draft Blocker

Keep the cold winter winds at bay by tucking this easy-to-knit draft blocker against the bottom of your door. The colorwash effect is created by alternating rows of color in a transition block between adjacent, related colors. Felting enhances the blended look. To give the draft blocker weight and stability, an inner liner is filled with inexpensive kitty litter.

YARN
Harrisville Designs Highland Style, 100% wool, worsted weight, 200 yd (183m)/3.5 oz (100g) skeins

mc   115 yds (105m)
     Peacock (#13)

cc A   60 yds (55m)
     Bluegrass (#70)

cc B   60 yds (55m)
     Loden Blue (#15)

cc C   115 yds (105m)
     Cobalt (#31)

cc D   110 yds (99m)
     Azure (#30)

NEEDLES
ONE SET of US #11 (8mm) double point needles, *or size you need to obtain gauge*

GAUGE, BEFORE FELTING
6 stitches = 2" (5cm), 7 rows = 2" (5cm) in stockinette stitch using two strands of yarn

NUMBER OF WASH CYCLES TO ACHIEVE SAMPLE SIZE
Two

OTHER SUPPLIES
Yarn needle; ¼ yd (23cm) liner fabric, 45" (113cm) wide; kitty litter (small bag); matching thread and needle

ABBREVIATIONS
cc   contrast color

mc   main color

APPROXIMATE MEASUREMENTS

Before Felting

4.5" (11.5cm) wide, 52" (1.3m) long

After Felting

3.5" (9cm) wide, 44" (1.2m) long

SET UP	Using 2 strands of mc, cast on 30 stitches. Divide stitches evenly among 3 needles; join. (For advice about knitting in the round, see page 173.)
NOTE	*Use double strands of each color yarn throughout.*
ROUNDS 1–12	Knit to end of each round.
ROUND 13, EYELET ROUND	*Knit 3, yarn over, knit 2 together; repeat from * to end of round. (For illustration of how to "yarn over," see page 174.)

Changing Colors

Do not cut yarns within the stripe sections, but be sure to twist the yarns around each other and to tug firmly on the new yarn each time you change colors.

ROUND 14	Knit to end of round, working each yarn over as a normal knit stitch.	
ROUNDS 15–20	Knit to end of each round.	
ROUNDS 21–26	Beginning with cc A, alternately knit 1 round of cc A and 1 round of mc for	6 rounds
ROUNDS 27–32	With cc A, knit to end of each round.	
ROUNDS 33–38	Beginning with cc B, alternately knit 1 round of cc B and 1 round of cc A for	6 rounds
ROUNDS 39–44	With cc B, knit to end of each round.	
ROUNDS 45–50	Beginning with cc C, alternately knit 1 round of cc C and 1 round of cc B for	6 rounds
ROUNDS 51–56	With cc C, knit to end of each round.	
ROUNDS 57–62	Beginning with cc D, alternately knit 1 round of cc D and 1 round of cc C for	6 rounds
ROUNDS 63–68	With cc D, knit to end of each round.	
ROUNDS 69–74	Beginning with cc C, alternately knit 1 round of cc C and 1 round of cc D for	6 rounds
ROUNDS 75–80	With cc C, knit to end of each round.	
ROUNDS 81–86	Beginning with cc D, alternately knit 1 round of cc D and 1 round of cc C for	6 rounds
ROUNDS 87–92	With cc D, knit to end of each round.	

ROUNDS 93–116	Repeat Rounds 69–92 one time.	
ROUNDS 117–122	Beginning with cc C, alternately knit 1 round of cc C and 1 round of cc D for	6 rounds
ROUNDS 123–128	With cc C, knit to end of each round.	
ROUNDS 129–134	Beginning with cc B, alternately knit 1 round of cc B and 1 round of cc C for	6 rounds
ROUNDS 135–140	With cc B, knit to end of each round.	
ROUNDS 141–146	Beginning with cc A, alternately knit 1 round of cc A and 1 round of cc B for	6 rounds
ROUNDS 147–152	With cc A, knit to end of each round.	
ROUNDS 153–158	Beginning with mc, alternately knit 1 round of mc and 1 round of cc A for	6 rounds
ROUNDS 159–164	With mc, knit to end of each round.	
ROUNDS 165–166	Repeat Rounds 13 and 14 (eyelet rounds).	
ROUNDS 167–178	Knit to end of each round. Bind off. Weave all loose ends into inside of draft blocker.	

FINISHING

With 1 strand of cc D, cast on 3 stitches and work a 25" (64cm) long I-cord (see page 171). Finish by knitting all 3 stitches together. Cut yarn, leaving a 10" (25cm) tail. Pull tail through remaining stitch; fasten off, then weave tail into center of cord. Weave in cast-on tail in same manner.

Felt blocker and I-cords together, following instructions on page 9. When felted as desired, smooth pieces on a flat surface. Avoid making hard creases along sides.

Measure blocker length between eyelet rows. Cut liner fabric to this length and double the width of blocker. Fold liner in half lengthwise, and machine stitch along length and one end. Slip liner inside blocker. Fill liner with kitty litter. Stitch open end closed. Using a yarn needle, re-open the eyelets, if necessary. Thread a felted I-cord through the eyelets on each end of blocker. Pull tight and tie in a bow.

Tea Cozy

Keep your teapot snug and warm with this brightly colored, whimsical cozy, decorated with small purple felt balls. You may have to trim the top edges of the cozy to get a smooth curve and a good match back and front, but the well- felted fabric will not ravel when you cut it. If you wish, knit one side of the cozy with the main color and the other side in one of the contrasting colors.

YARN
Brown Sheep Lamb's Pride, 85% wool/15% mohair, worsted weight, 190 yd (174m)/4 oz (114g) skeins

mc   210 yds (189m)
    Lotus Pink (#M38)

cc A   30 yds (26m)
    Blue Boy (#M79)

cc B   20 yds (18m)
    Aztec Turquoise (#M78)

cc C   20 yds (18m)
    Limeade (#M120)

NEEDLES
ONE PAIR US #11 (8mm) straight needles, *or size you need to obtain gauge*

GAUGE, BEFORE FELTING
7 stitches = 2" (5cm), 8 rows = 2" (5cm) in stockinette stitch

NUMBER OF WASH CYCLES TO ACHIEVE SAMPLE SIZE
Two

OTHER SUPPLIES
Yarn needle, matching sewing thread and needle, purple fleece for seven felt balls, marking pen

ABBREVIATIONS

cc   contrast color

mc   main color

APPROXIMATE MEASUREMENTS

Before Felting

15" (38cm) wide, 16" (40m) tall

After Felting

11" (28cm) wide, 10" (26cm) tall

KNITTING THE BODY

NOTE	Instructions are for one side. Make 2 bodies (front and back) exactly the same.
SET UP	Using a single strand of cc A, cast on 50 stitches for the garter stitch (knit every row) band.
ROWS 1–8	Knit to end of each row. Cut cc A, leaving a 10" (25cm) tail to weave in on the inside.
ROW 9	Join mc. Knit to end of row.
ROW 10	Purl to end of row.
NEXT ROWS	Continue to knit 1 row, purl 1 row (stockinette stitch) until piece measures 12½" (32cm). End at the completion of a purl row.

DECREASING TO THE TOP

ROW 1	Knit 2 together, knit to end of row. *You now have* 49 stitches.
ROW 2	Purl 2 together, purl to end of row. *You now have* 48 stitches.
ROWS 3–20	Repeat Rows 1 and 2. *You now have* 30 stitches.
	Bind off. Weave in all loose ends.

KNITTING THE POINTS

NOTE	Make 4 points using cc B and 4 points using cc C.
SET UP	With cc B or cc C, cast on 15 stitches.
ROW 1	Purl to end of row.
ROW 2	Knit 2 together, knit until 2 stitches remain, knit 2 together. *You now have* 13 stitches.
ROW 3	Purl to end of row.
ROWS 4–13	Repeat Rows 2-3. *You now have* 3 stitches.

Cut yarn, leaving a tail 10 inches (25cm) long. Thread tail through yarn needle and draw yarn through remaining stitches. Fasten off. Weave in all loose ends.

FINISHING

Felt all pieces, following the instructions on page 9.

Lay the wet, felted pieces on a flat surface, and stretch and smooth them, making sure they lay flat. Pin them in place and allow them to dry thoroughly. Arrange the points so that they are flat. Allow them to dry. (See illustrations, page 11.)

FELTING THE BALLS

Follow the instructions on page 157 for making felt balls. Make the size as consistent as possible, about ¾" (2cm) in diameter.

ASSEMBLING THE TEA COZY

If necessary, trim the upper edges of the cozy front and back to create a smooth curve. Lay the front and back pieces together and trim as needed to make them identical.

Place one cozy piece (the back) wrong side up on a table. With the points right side up, evenly space them around the outer edge of the cozy, beginning and ending just above the lower border, and alternating colors as shown in the photo on page 152. Use a permanent marking pen to mark the outer edges of each point on the wrong side of the cozy back.

Keeping the points inside the markings, slide them down so that the bottom edges of the points overlap the top edge of the cozy approximately ¼ inch (.6cm). With matching thread, use tiny whipstitches to sew the points in place. Turn the cozy over, so that the right side is up, and use tiny whipstitches to reinforce the other side. (See illustration on following page.)

Take the remaining cozy piece (the front) and place it against the back with wrong sides together. Pin or tack the pieces together between each of the points. Use small whipstitches to sew the cozy front to the cozy back. Pull the stitches tightly so that they are buried in the felted fabric and don't show. If the stitching shows on the right side of the cozy, use a small brush (such as a pet brush or a toothbrush) to gently brush the area around the stitches.

Attach a felt ball to the cozy between each of the points, using matching sewing thread.

Attaching the triangles to the inside of the back

Sewing the front to the back

Making Felt Balls

6 EASY STEPS

MATERIALS

Liquid dishwashing soap or laundry detergent

8½ cups warm water

White vinegar

2-quart, 1-pint, and 1-cup containers

Washed and combed wool fleece

1. **PREPARING SOLUTIONS.** In the 2-quart container, combine ¼ cup soap with 6 cups warm water. In the 1-pint container, combine ½ cup soap with 1½ cups warm water. Stir 2 tablespoons white vinegar into 1 cup water.

2. **GETTING STARTED.** Take a small handful of fleece about twice as big as the finished ball, and divide it in half. Separate one half into several small bundles. Fluff out and align the fibers of these bundles. *Tip:* For equal-sized balls, prepare enough fleece for all the balls you plan to make before you begin the felting process.

3. **WETTING THE CORE.** Dip the unseparated fleece into the weak soap solution, squeezing it until it is fully saturated.

4. **WRAP IT UP.** Firmly wrap one of the fleece bundles around the saturated fleece. Smooth it as you wrap, taking care not to pinch or twist the bundle. Dip the ball into the stronger soap solution to wet the outer layer. Add the remaining bundles, smoothing and wetting them in the same manner. *Tip:* Use your palms rather than your fingertips.

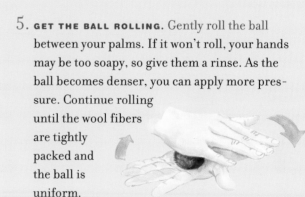

5. **GET THE BALL ROLLING.** Gently roll the ball between your palms. If it won't roll, your hands may be too soapy, so give them a rinse. As the ball becomes denser, you can apply more pressure. Continue rolling until the wool fibers are tightly packed and the ball is uniform.

6. **FINISHING UP.** Rinse the ball under hot water and then drop it in the vinegar solution for a few seconds (this restores the pH of the wool). Roll the ball again to remove excess moisture and reshape it. Allow it to air dry.

Tropical Stripes Oven Set

There'll be no burned fingers or scorched counter tops when you use these coordinating, brightly striped oven accessories. Use double-strands of worsted yarn for the protective thickness, or choose a bulky weight yarn for the same effect.

YARN
Brown Sheep Lamb's Pride, 85% wool/15% mohair, worsted weight, 190 yd (173m)/4 oz (113g) skeins

mc   65 yds (52m)
       Aztec Turquoise (M 78)

cc A   65 yds (52m)
       Brite Blue (M 57)

cc B   100 yds (90m)
       Christmas Green (M 165)

cc C   165 yds (150m)
       Blue Boy (M 79)

cc D   120 yds (108m)
       Supreme Purple (M 100)

cc E   50 yds (45m)
       Limeade (M 120)

NEEDLES
ONE SET US #15 (10mm) double point needles, *or size you need to obtain gauge*
ONE PAIR US #15 (10mm) straight needles, *or size you need to obtain gauge*
ONE SET US #10 ½ (6.5mm) double point needles, for I-cord

GAUGE
5 stitches = 2" (5cm), 7 rows = 2" (5cm) with two strands of yarn in stockinette stitch

NUMBER OF WASH CYCLES TO ACHIEVE SAMPLE SIZE
Three

OTHER SUPPLIES
Yarn needle, stitch holder, 2 stitch markers

ABBREVIATIONS
cc   contrast color
mc   main color

APPROXIMATE MEASUREMENTS

	Before Felting:	After Felting:
OVEN MITT	17" (43cm) tall, 7" (18cm) wide	11" (28cm) tall, 5½" (14cm) wide
POT HOLDER AND HOT PAD	10½" (27cm) wide, 11" (28cm) tall	8½" (22cm) square

SET UP	Holding 2 strands of mc together, use US #15 (10 mm) double point needles to cast on 36 stitches. Divide the stitches evenly among three needles; join. (For information about knitting in the round, see page 173.)
NOTE	Use a double strand of each color throughout.
ROUNDS 1–10	Knit to end of each round.
ROUND 11	Change to cc A. Knit 2, place a stitch marker on the needle, make 1 (see page 172), knit 1, make 1, place a stitch marker on the needle, knit to end of round. *You now have* 38 stitches (3 stitches between markers).
ROUND 12	Knit to end of round.
ROUND 13	Knit 2, slide marker, make 1, knit to next stitch marker, make 1, slide stitch marker, knit to end of round. *You now have* 40 stitches (5 stitches between markers).
ROUNDS 14–20	Repeat Rounds 12 and 13.
ROUNDS 21–25	Change to cc B. Repeat Rounds 12 and 13. After Round 25 you have 52 stitches (17 stitches between markers).
ROUNDS 26–29	Knit to the end of each round.
ROUND 30	Knit 2, remove marker, slide the 17 stitches onto a stitch holder, remove marker, cast on 1 stitch, knit to end of round. *You now have* 36 stitches.
ROUNDS 31–40	Change to cc C. Knit to end of each round.
ROUNDS 41–50	Change to cc D. Knit to end of each round.

DECREASING FOR THE TOP OF THE MITT

ROUND 1	Change to cc E. *Knit 4, knit 2 together; repeat from * to end of round. *You now have* 30 stitches.
ROUND 2	Knit to end of round.

ROUND 3	*Knit 3, knit 2 together; repeat from * to end of round. *You now have* 24 stitches.
ROUND 4	Knit to end of round.
ROUND 5	*Knit 2, knit 2 together; repeat from * to end of round. *You now have* 18 stitches.
ROUND 6	Knit to end of round.
ROUND 7	*Knit 1, knit 2 together; repeat from * to end of round. *You now have* 12 stitches.
ROUND 8	Knit to end of round.
ROUND 9	*Knit 2 together; repeat from * to end of round. *You now have* 6 stitches.
	Cut yarn, leaving a 12" (30cm) tail of yarn. Thread tail through a yarn needle and draw yarn through the remaining stitches. Fasten off.

KNITTING THE THUMB

SET UP	Divide the stitches from the holder among three needles, as follows: Needle 1: 6 stitches Needle 2: 7 stitches Needle 3: 4 stitches
	Using cc B, and starting with Needle 1, knit to end of round, then use Needle 3 to pick up and knit 3 more stitches across the opening. *You now have* 20 stitches.
ROUND 1	Change to cc C. Knit to end of round.
ROUND 2	Knit 8, knit 2 together, knit 8, knit 2 together. *You now have* 18 stitches.
ROUNDS 3–10	Knit to end of each round.
ROUND 11	*Knit 1, knit 2 together; repeat from * to end of round. *You now have* 12 stitches.
ROUND 12	Knit to end of round.

| ROUND 13 | *Knit 2 together; repeat from * to end of round. *You now have* 6 stitches. | | |
| | Cut yarn, leaving a 12" (30cm) tail of yarn. Thread tail through a yarn needle, and draw yarn through the remaining stitches. Fasten off. Weave in the tail on the inside of the mitt. Weave in any other loose ends. | | |

KNITTING THE I-CORD HANGING LOOP FOR THE OVEN MITT

With 1 strand of cc E and smaller double point needles cast on 3 stitches. Following instructions on page 171, knit a 5" (12.5cm) long I-cord. Bring yarn across back of work and knit all 3 stitches together. Cut yarn, leaving a 10" (25cm) tail. Thread tail through a yarn needle, and sew the I-cord into a loop. With remaining tail, sew I-cord loop to one corner of mitt. Weave this tail into center of cord.

KNITTING THE POTHOLDER AND HOT POT PAD

		HOT POT PAD	POTHOLDER
NOTE	Knit potholder and hot pot pad with 2 strands of yarn throughout. When you change colors, cut the old yarn, leaving a 5" (12.5cm) tail. Thread tails through a yarn needle and weave them in as you go, or catch them with working yarn for 8-10 stitches on wrong side.		
SET UP	Using the straight needles, cast on 25 stitches, using 2 strands of	mc	cc A
ROW 1	Knit to end of row. Turn.		
ROW 2	Purl to end of row. Turn.		
ROWS 3–10	Repeat Rows 1 and 2.		
ROW 11	Change yarns (see at right), and knit to end of row. Turn.	cc B	cc B
ROW 12	Purl to end of row. Turn.		
ROWS 13–20	Repeat Rows 11 and 12.		
ROW 21	Change yarns (see at right), and knit to end of row. Turn.	cc E	cc D

		HOT POT PAD	POTHOLDER
ROW 22	Purl to end of row. Turn.		
ROWS 23–30	Repeat Rows 21 and 22.		
ROW 31	Change yarns (see at right), and knit to end of row. Turn.	cc C	cc C
ROW 32	Purl to end of row. Turn.		
ROWS 33–40	Repeat Rows 31 and 32.		
	Bind off. Cut yarn, leaving a 10" (25cm) tail. Thread the tail through a yarn needle and weave in the yarn on the wrong side of the potholder. Weave in any other loose ends before felting.		

KNITTING THE I-CORD HANGING LOOP FOR POTHOLDER

SET UP	Using 1 strand of cc B, follow the instructions for knitting the I-cord hanging loop for the oven mitt (opposite). Attach the loop to one corner of the potholder.

FINISHING

Felt all 3 projects together, following the directions on page 9. During agitation, check frequently, removing items from lingerie bag and stretching them to keep the stripes and edges even.

When items are felted as desired, smooth and flatten the oven mitt, stretching the bottom edge so that the stripes are even. Stretch the pot holder and hot pot pad so that corners are square and edges and stripes are even. Pin in place to hold shape during drying period.

Furry Top Christmas Stocking

You'll love knitting these nifty stockings, and Santa will love filling them to the brim. The secret to the furry tops is a strand of brushed mohair worked along with the worsted wool.

YARN

mc   Brown Sheep Lamb's Pride, 85% wool/15% mohair, worsted weight, 190 yd (174m)/4 oz (114g) skeins

Sapphire (#M65)

Small: 75 yds (68m)

Large: 150 yds (135m)

cc A   Manos del Uruguay, 100% wool, 135 yd (122m)/3.5 oz (100g) skeins

Olive (#55)

Small: 35 yds (32m)

Large: 55 yds (50m)

cc B   Rowan Kidsilk Haze, 70% kid mohair/30% silk, 227 yd (204m)/.88 oz (25g) balls

Jelly (#597)

Small: 10 yds (9m)

Large: 15 yds (14m)

NEEDLES

ONE SET US #15 (10mm) double point needles, *or size you need to obtain gauge*

GAUGE, BEFORE FELTING

7 stitches = 2" (5cm), 8 rows = 2" (5cm) using single strand of mc in stockinette stitch

SIZES

Small and Large

NUMBER OF WASH CYCLES TO ACHIEVE SAMPLE SIZE

Three

OTHER SUPPLIES

Yarn needle, stitch holder (optional)

ABBREVIATIONS

cc   contrast color

mc   main color

APPROXIMATE MEASUREMENTS

	Before Felting	After Felting
SMALL	22" (55cm) long	13" (33cm) long
LARGE	28" (70cm) long	17" (43cm) long

KNITTING THE CUFF

		SMALL	LARGE
SET UP	Holding one strand of cc A and one strand of cc B together, cast on	24 stitches	36 stitches
	Divide the stitches evenly among three needles. Join, being careful not to twist stitches. For advice about knitting in the round, see page 173.		
	Knit to the end of each round for	8 rounds	10 rounds
	Cut cc A and cc B, leaving a 10" (25cm) tail to weave in later.		

KNITTING THE LEG

		SMALL	LARGE
	Change to mc. Knit to the end of each round until leg from the bottom of the cuff measures	10" (26cm)	14" (36cm)

KNITTING THE HEEL FLAP

		SMALL	LARGE
NOTE	You will be working back and forth in stockinette stitch (knit one row, purl one row) in this section.		
SET UP	From Needle 1, knit	6 stitches	9 stitches
	Slide from Needle 1 to Needle 2 the remaining	2 stitches	3 stitches
	Slide from Needle 3 to Needle 1	6 stitches	9 stitches
	Slide from Needle 3 to Needle 2 the remaining	2 stitches	3 stitches
	Set Needle 3 (now empty) aside. You can put the stitches that are now on Needle 2 on a stitch holder or leave them on Needle 2 until you need to work on them again.		
	The stitches are distributed as follows:		
	Needle 1:	12 stitches	18 stitches
	Needle 2:	12 stitches	18 stitches

		SMALL	LARGE
ROW 1 (WRONG SIDE)	Change to cc A. Turn so that you are working on the wrong side. Slip 1 stitch and then purl to end of row. Turn.		
ROW 2	Slip 1 stitch, knit to end of row. Turn.		
ROW 3	Slip 1 stitch, purl to end of row. Turn.		
	Repeat Rows 2-3	3 more times	4 more times
	End at the completion of a purl row:	Row 9	Row 11
NOTE	In the next section, directions for Small and Large sizes are given separately.		

TURNING THE HEEL, SMALL SIZE ONLY

ROW 1	Slip 1 stitch, knit 5, knit 2 together, knit 1. Turn, leaving 3 stitches unworked.
ROW 2	Slip 1 stitch, purl 1, purl 2 together, purl 1. Turn, leaving 3 stitches unworked.
ROW 3	Slip 1 stitch, knit 2, knit 2 together, knit 1. Turn, leaving 1 stitch unworked.
ROW 4	Slip 1 stitch, purl 3, purl 2 together, purl 1. Turn, leaving 1 stitch unworked.
ROW 5	Slip 1 stitch, knit 4, knit 2 together. Turn. (All stitches on this side are now worked.)
ROW 6	Slip 1 stitch, purl 4, purl 2 together. Turn. *You now have 6 "live" stitches on the needle.*

TURNING THE HEEL, LARGE SIZE ONLY

ROW 1	Slip 1 stitch, knit 9, knit 2 together, knit 1. Turn, leaving 5 stitches unworked.

		SMALL	LARGE
ROW 2	Slip 1 stitch, purl 3, purl 2 together, purl 1. Turn, leaving 5 stitches unworked.		
ROW 3	Slip 1 stitch, knit 4, knit 2 together, knit 1. Turn, leaving 3 stitches unworked.		
ROW 4	Slip 1 stitch, purl 5, purl 2 together, purl 1. Turn, leaving 3 stitches unworked		
ROW 5	Slip 1 stitch, knit 6, knit 2 together, knit 1. Turn, leaving 1 stitch unworked.		
ROW 6	Slip 1 stitch, purl 7, purl 2 together, purl 1. Turn, leaving 1 stitch unworked.		
ROW 7	Slip 1 stitch, knit 8, knit 2 together. Turn. (All stitches on this side are now worked.)		
ROW 8	Slip 1 stitch, purl 8 stitches, purl 2 together. Turn. *You now have* 10 "live" stitches on the needle.		

KNITTING THE GUSSET

		SMALL	LARGE
NOTE	In this section, you will again be knitting in the round.		
ROUND 1	Slip 1 stitch, knit from heel flap	2 stitches	4 stitches
	This needle is now Needle 3.		
	Cut cc A, leaving a 10" (25cm) tail to weave in later.		
	Change to mc and with an empty needle, knit from the heel flap the remaining	3 stitches	5 stitches
	With the same needle (now called Needle 1), pick up along the side of the heel flap	8 stitches	10 stitches
	Go back to the stitches that you left on Needle 2 in Knitting the Heel Flap, above, and knit to end of needle.	(12 stitches)	(18 stitches)

	SMALL	LARGE
Use an empty needle to pick up along the other side of the heel flap	8 stitches	10 stitches
Using this same needle, knit Needle 3's remaining	3 stitches	5 stitches
The stitches are now distributed as follows:		
Needle 1:	11 stitches	15 stitches
Needle 2:	12 stitches	18 stitches
Needle 3:	11 stitches	15 stitches

ROUND 2   Knit to end of round.

ROUND 3   Needle 1: Knit to the last 2 stitches, knit 2 together.

Needle 2: Knit to end of needle.

Needle 3: Knit 2 together, knit to end of needle.

	SMALL	LARGE
You now have (Needle 1/Needle 2/Needle 3)	32 stitches (10/12/10)	46 stitches (14/18/14)
NEXT ROUNDS Repeat Rounds 2 and 3 until Needles 1 and 3 each contain	6 stitches	9 stitches
You now have	24 stitches	36 stitches

KNITTING THE FOOT

SET UP   Redistribute the stitches evenly among the three needles.

	SMALL	LARGE
FOOT ROUNDS Knit to end of each round until foot, from where the gusset ends, measures	6" (15cm)	7" (18cm)

Cut mc, leaving a 10" (25 cm) tail to weave in later.

DECREASING FOR THE TOE: LARGE SIZE ONLY

NOTE   Size Large needs 4 extra rounds to decrease the toe.

	SMALL	LARGE
ROUND 1 Change to cc A. *Knit 4, knit 2 together; repeat from * to end of round. *You now have*	——	30 stitches

		SMALL	LARGE
ROUNDS 2 AND 4	Knit to end of each round.		
ROUND 3	*Knit 3, knit 2 together; repeat from * to end of round. *You now have*	—	24 stitches

DECREASING FOR THE TOE, BOTH SIZES

		SMALL	LARGE
ROUND 1	*Knit 2, knit 2 together; repeat from * to end of round. *You now have*	18 stitches	18 stitches
ROUNDS 2 AND 4	Knit to end of each round.		
ROUND 3	*Knit 1, knit 2 together; repeat from * to end of round. *You now have*	12 stitches	12 stitches
ROUND 5	*Knit 2 together; repeat from * to end of round. *You now have*	6 stitches	6 stitches

Cut yarn, leaving a 12" (30cm) tail. Thread tail through a yarn needle, and draw yarn through the remaining stitches on the needle. Fasten off. Draw yarn to the inside of the stocking and weave in tail on the wrong side. Weave in any other loose ends.

KNITTING THE I-CORD HANGING LOOP

Using cc A, cast on 3 stitches. Following instructions on page 171, knit a 5" (12.5cm) long I-cord. Knit all 3 stitches together. Fasten off. Cut yarn, leaving a 10" (25cm) tail. Thread tail through a yarn needle and draw yarn into cord. Thread remaining tail through a yarn needle, fold loop in half and use tail to stitch ends together and to upper outside edge of stocking cuff. Weave in tail on wrong side.

FINISHING

Following the instructions on page 9, felt the stocking to the degree desired. Smooth and flatten the stocking, stretching to get it even all around. Allow it to dry completely. Brush the mohair cuff to raise and heighten its fuzziness.

Knitting Terms Defined

ASTERISK (*): Repeat directions contained between asterisks, often across the row. For example, if you have 12 stitches and the directions say, "*Knit 2, knit 2 together; repeat from * to end of row," you will work the sequence "knit 2, knit 2 together" three times.

CAST OFF: Casting off (sometimes called binding off) is a technique for taking the stitches off the needle so that the knitting does not unravel. Here's a general-purpose cast-off: Knit 2 stitches, then draw the first stitch over the second and slip it off the needle. Knit the next stitch and draw the second stitch over it. Repeat until all stitches are bound off. Cut the tail of yarn and thread it through the remaining stitch and tighten it. (See also Three-Needle Cast Off.)

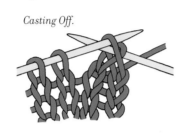

Casting Off.

CAST ON: The long-tail cast on makes a neat, firm, but elastic edge: Estimate length of "tail" by wrapping yarn around needle one time for each cast-on stitch you need. Make a slip knot right here, and slide knot over a knitting needle. Hold needle in your right hand; hold tail over thumb and working end of yarn over index finger of your left hand (Step 1). Insert needle under front loop of tail on your thumb. Bring needle over and behind working yarn on index finger (Step 2). Use nee-

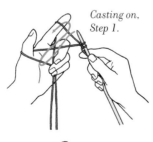

Casting on, Step 1.

Casting on, Step 2.

dle to draw working yarn through loop on your thumb; release loop. Place thumb under tail, and draw yarns toward you holding both firmly.

DECREASE: A decrease reduces the total stitch number by one. For the purposes of this book, a decrease is worked by knitting (or purling) 2 stitches together.

Decreasing by knitting 2 together.

FAIR ISLE KNITTING: Fair Isle (also known as stranded) knitting creates patterns by using more than one color in a row. Traditional patterns usually have no more than two colors in a single row. The color sequence is indicated by a chart on which each stitch is represented by a colored square. Follow the charts, line by line, beginning at the bottom right. For projects worked in the round, read each line of the chart from right to left. For projects worked on straight needles in stockinette stitch, read right-side (knit) rows from right to left, and wrong-side (purl) rows from left to right. Carry unused yarn loosely across back of work. It is especially important to keep loose tension on non-working yarn when you are knitting projects to be felted, since yarns that are carried too tightly shrink disproportionately and distort the shape of felted items. Never carry yarn more than three stitches without catching it with working yarn.

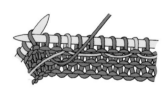

Carrying a second color.

I-CORD: An I-cord is a narrow tube knitted with two double point needles on 3 or 4 stitches. Your pattern will tell you how many stitches to use. If you knit the cord separately from the main item, you will cast on these stitches. In some cases (on purses, for example) you may be asked to pick up stitches from the finished knitting (the top edge, for instance) to begin the I-cord. This makes a stronger join than simply sewing the cord to the item. To make an I-cord, cast on (or pick up) 3 (or 4) stitches; knit 3 (or 4). Do not turn, but move the needle holding the stitches to your left hand. Slide the stitches to the right end of the needle, so that the first cast-on stitch is the first stitch at the tip of the left needle. Insert the right needle, knitwise, into that stitch, bring the yarn from the left to the right across the back of the knitting, and knit the stitch in the usual manner. Make sure you knit the first stitch tightly. Knit the remaining stitches on the needle. Repeat this procedure until the I-cord is the desired length.

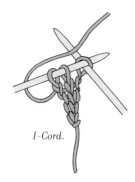

I-Cord.

INCREASE: An increase adds one stitch to the total stitch number. Some projects, use the increase method known as "make 1." (See drawing at left). Look for the horizontal bar between the first stitch on your left needle and the last stitch on your right needle. With the tip of your left needle, pick up this bar from back to front. Knit into the bar from the front, which twists the new stitch and gives it a slant to the right. Even though it may seem a bit tricky to get your needle into the bar from front to back, it's important to do so in order to avoid creating a small hole in the fabric.

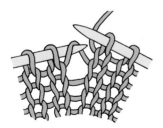

Increase by "make 1."

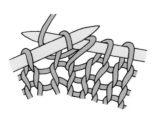

Increase by knitting into front and back of stitch.

Some patterns suggest increasing by knitting first into the front and then into the back of the same stitch before dropping it off the needle (see drawing, bottom left).

INTARSIA: To prepare for intarsia knitting, wind several small bobbins (available at yarn shops) with the yarn you'll be using. When you begin each new color, wrap the new yarn around the old before leaving the old behind. This locks the yarns neatly together and creates a strong, smooth join with no gaps. Be sure to make the interlock on the wrong side of the work on both knit and purl rows.

Intarsia.

JOIN NEW YARN: When you need to change colors for stripes or Fair Isle patterns or to begin a new ball of yarn, you'll find that every knitter has a favorite way of making the join. We recommend working the new tail in on the wrong side of the piece for the last 6 or 7 stitches before it's needed, by catching it under the working yarn. Then, when you change yarns, leave a 3-inch (7.5 cm) tail of the old yarn that you can work in in the same manner. If you wish, you can also just leave the tails hanging and weave them in later, before felting.

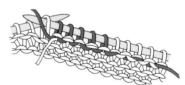

Joining a strand of new yarn (turquoise strand).

KITCHENER STITCH: This clever technique allows you to join two knitted pieces almost invisibly. With stitches on needles, hold two fabric layers together with wrong sides together. Using a yarn needle, draw yarn through first stitch of front needle as if to knit;

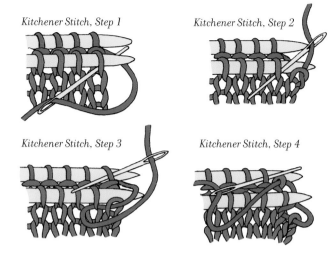

Kitchener Stitch, Step 1

Kitchener Stitch, Step 2

Kitchener Stitch, Step 3

Kitchener Stitch, Step 4

slip stitch off (step 1). Draw yarn through second stitch of front needle as if to purl; leave stitch on needle (step 2). Draw yarn through first stitch of back needle as if to purl; slip stitch off (step 3). Draw yarn through second stitch of back needle as if to knit; leave stitch on (step 4). Repeat steps until no stitches remain on needles.

KNITTING IN THE ROUND: In order to knit a seamless tube (for some slippers, hats, and bags, for instance), you must join a row of stitches in to a circle and knit "in the round" on double point or circular needles.

When using double point needles, divide the stitches evenly among three needles. Form the needles into a triangle, making sure that the stitches are not twisted on the needles. With a fourth needle and the yarn from the third needle, knit the first stitch on

Joining in the round on double point needles.

the first needle. When you have knitted all the stitches on one needle, use the newly empty needle to knit the stitches on the next needle. Never turn and work in the opposite direction.

When knitting on a circular needle, use the working yarn from the right needle to knit the first stitch on the left needle. Slide the stitches around on the cable as you knit. It is a good idea to slip a stitch marker on the needle at the beginning of the round, so that you can easily see where the next round begins.

PICK UP STITCHES: Slide the point of the left needle into an existing loop. Knit that loop as a stitch. You will need to pick up stitches along the base edges of a bag and along the heel flap to form the gusset of a slipper and to close the gap between the thumb and the rest of the oven mitt (page 161).

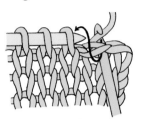

Using a crochet needle to pick up stitches.

ROUND: All stitches worked once when you are knitting circularly on double point or circular needles.

ROW: All stitches worked once across a straight needle.

STOCKINETTE STITCH: When working "flat," stockinette stitch is formed by knitting all of the stitches on the right side of the work, and purling all of the stitches on the wrong side of the work. When working in the round, stockinette stitch is formed by knitting all the stitches (the work is not turned).

TAIL: The excess yarn left when stitches are cast on, or the excess yarn left when stitches are bound off. The tail is often used to weave stitches together or to sew openings closed. Weave tails in on inside of work.

THREE-NEEDLE CAST OFF: This is a useful technique if you want to cast off and at the same time join two pieces in an invisible seam, such as at the bottom of a purse. Place half the stitches on one needle and half on a second needle. If you are using straight, single-point needles, make sure their tips are pointing in the same direction. Bring the two pieces, or two

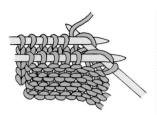

Three-needle cast off.

halves, together with the right sides facing. Beginning at the outer edge, insert a third needle through the first stitch on the front and back needles and knit them together. Make a second stitch in the same way. Pass the first stitch over the second one. Continue in this manner until all stitches are cast off. Draw the tail of yarn through the remaining stitch and fasten securely.

TURN: Turn needle around and work across the other side of the work. When knitting with straight needles, turn work at the end of every row. When knitting with double point needles, turn work only when specifically instructed (when knitting the heel flap or turning the heel on a slipper, for example).

WEAVE ENDS IN: Thread the tail in a yarn needle and sew the end through a few stitches on the back of the work. Cut the excess tail.

WHIPSTITCH: An overcast stitch used to sew the outside edges of two pieces of fabric together.

YARN OVER: Wrap the yarn completely around the needle before working the next stitch. For the purposes of this book, a "yarn over" forms an eyelet.

Acknowledgments

Without Stacey Glick's unflagging support, and Gwen Steege's guidance, this book would not have come to be. I am happy to have this opportunity to thank them both.

I am deeply grateful for the continued support of the usual cheerleading staff, joined this time around by Knitters Etc., and the Prairie Arts Fiber Guild, who weathered the ups and downs along with me.

And as always, I am thankful for Terry, who cheerfully endured months in a house full of wet wool.

IN APPRECIATION OF THEIR ADVICE AND ENCOURAGEMENT, THANKS TO:

Leslie Voiers, color consulting
Barbara Elkins and the staff at WEBS, Northampton, MA
Rae Yurek and the staff at Harrisville Designs, Harrisville, NH

AND MANY THANKS TO:

The yarn companies who supplied yarn:
Brown Sheep Company, Mitchell, NE (www.brownsheep.com)
Classic Elite, Lowell, MA
Halcyon Yarn, Bath, ME (www.halcyonyarn.com)
Harrisville Designs, Harrisville, NH (www.harrisville.com)
Morehouse Farm, Milan, NY (www.morehousemerino.com)
Nordic Fiber Arts, Durham, NH (www.nordicfiberarts.com)

The profiled artists:
Crispina ffrench (www.crispina.com), Beverly Galeskas (www.fibertrends.com), Heather Kerner, Kristiane Kristensen, Cindy Walker (www.stonyhillfiberarts.com)

The knitters:
Gigi Bass, Rebecca Bien, Kathleen Case, Colleen Conlan, Leslie Reed Evans, Diana Foster, Lissa Greenough, Mary Johnson, Alison Kolesar, Ruth Ann Myers, Kathy Oliverson, Carolynn Vincent

Index

Numbers in *italic* are photos and illustrations, numbers in **bold** are pattern instructions.